ALMOST THERE

The Autobiography
Of an Artist

Author
Darryl T. Easley

Almost There Copyright © 2016 by Darryl T. Easley and World Movement Publishing. All rights reserved. Printed in the United States of America. No part of this book may be used or reproduced in any manner whatsoever, stored in a retrieval system, data base or transmitted, in any form or by any means—electronic, mechanical, photocopying, recording or otherwise – without prior written permission of the publisher.

For information contact:
World Movement Publishing
409 N. Pacific Coast Highway, Suite 417
Redondo Beach, CA 90277
info@worldmovement.com and website: www.worldmovement.com

Library of Congress Control Number   2016943209
ISBN 10: 0-9828768-5-8
ISBN 13: 978-0-9828768-5-5

World Movement Publishing books may be purchased for educational, business, or sales promotional use. For information please contact:
World Movement Publishing
409 N. Pacific Coast Highway, Suite 417
Redondo Beach, CA 90277
info@worldmovement.com and website: www.worldmovement.com

This book is a work based on a true story. Some names, characters, places, and incidents have been changed to protect the innocent and any resemblance to actual persons, living or dead, businesses, companies, events or locales are entirely coincidental.

Cover design by Elegant Stylz Portraits, Ms. Kym Russell

THIS BOOK IS DEDICATED TO MY PARENTS
FOR ALL YOUR LOVE AND SUPPORT THROUGHOUT
THE YEARS…
I LOVE AND MISS YOU BOTH…..R.I.P

Leona Easley & Ronald T. Easley

ACKNOWLEDGEMENTS

I'd like to begin by giving thanks to God for blessing me with vision and creativity to write my life experience. When I first sat down to put pen to paper, my goal was to educate up and coming entertainers on the do's and don'ts of the music industry by sharing my experiences. This book has truly been a journey…a labor…and therapy. Those of you closest to me know this. For those of you reading this for the first time, I hope you enjoy and appreciate that this journey has contributed to molding me into the man I am today. Thanks for sharing my journey.

Thanks to...

Lamont Patterson, Olivia Shannon and World Movement Publishing for allowing me the opportunity to share my story with the world.

Terri Johnson and Brigitte Harris for allowing me the opportunity to work on the book synopsis with my Spoken Word piece and for my role in the upcoming Movie "Rape" Initial Shock The Brigitte Harris Story.

Kym Russell, for all of your dedication, hard work and support throughout the years. For creating my book cover. Your photos, graphic designs, videos and ideas have been on point. When I make it, you make it. You're loved and greatly appreciated.

Rhonda Easley, Kevin Easley, Renee Easley, Keana& Kesha Thompson, Christina Moore-Easley, Andrew Bailey, Dymond McCallum, De'aira Easley, Bryant Bentley, Brian Ragsdale, Mary Summers, Antonio Williams,Tony Jackson, Marci Baker, Michelle Simmons, Traci Davis, C. Brooks, Ruby Harris, Bridgitte Gamble, Lee Johnson, Gary Wallace, Kenny "Herk" Norman, Lamar "DJ Mix" Moody, Rob "Big Rob" Moore, John "Buster" Lewis, Velvis "2-Pot" Priest, Robert Henderson, Reggie Moon, Devin Christopher, Darrell Y-Tank" Thomas, Russell Pryor, Aunt Juanita Wallace, David Wallace, Aunt Mary Harper, Robert Harper, Fee Fee, Monica, Delilah, Sade, Perry, Juan,Jan Lewis, Michelle Brewer, Christopher Nolan. My Omega Church Family.

To my Grandmother, Geraldine Smith, I love you more than words can say!

TABLE OF CONTENTS

Beginning of the End 1

The Big Move to Cali 13

Long Ride Home 27

The Rise and Fall of Bullseye Records 31

First Song on the Radio 65

Star Trak Records 71

Roger & Larry Troutman 89

Thoughts on the Industry 107

Reflections 111

New Beginning 113

BEGINNING OF THE END

I first started my relationship with Hip Hop well over 2 decades ago. I guess you can say that Hip Hop and I had a love-hate relationship. At one time, I really, really loved it. I ate, slept, thought and shit Hip Hop. I also hated it, and at some point began to wonder why I even started a relationship with it. Just like a Man-Woman relationship, I began to fall out of love with it. I didn't just fall out of love with it. At least, not until it hurt me, betrayed me, and used me to the point that I felt really stupid.

So after 20 years in this love-hate relationship, I have decided to leave. After reading this book, you will understand the struggle, the joy, and the pain I endured while having this affiliation with Hip Hop.

The first time I fell in love with Hip Hop was in 1979 when I first heard Kurtis Blow's "The Breaks". I begged my mother to buy me the 12 inch record. After convincing her to purchase the record, I wrote each and every word and learned the entire song. It wasn't easy either, because the record was on a record player. Therefore, I had to listen to a few words and then pull the needle off the 12 inch record and write what I had heard and then put the needle back on the record and listen some more. You see, record players didn't have a stop and rewind.

Another artist I enjoyed listening to back in 1980-81 was a guy that no one ever gives credit to. His name was King

Tim III. He rapped with a group called the Fatback Band. After that song blew me away, I started writing my own raps. They were corny as hell, but it was the beginning of me discovering my talent in the early '80's and learning to utilize my talent as a writer.

One of my main goals with this book is to educate up-and-coming artist. Whether it is a rapper, a singer, a producer or even a writer, there's nothing wrong with having a dream of becoming a major star. But, what I want understood is that you should never put all your eggs in one basket. What I mean by that is…don't bank on it happening. Do other things with your talent just in case it never happens. I'm not trying to discourage anyone. I don't want anyone to make the same mistake I made in this game and that's what the music industry is…a major game. The players are the Artists. Then you have the coaches. The coaches are record company Presidents. And finally, you have the owners. The owners are the C.E.O's. You follow me? The players are paid to play, and while the players are playing their hearts out, they're acquiring riches, fame and respect.

There's nothing the organization won't do while you're playing well. If after sometime the player stops playing so well, the owner tells the coach to cut the

player and look for another player to replace him. After that happens, you no longer have the riches, fame or respect from that organization. Translation… when the Artist is selling enough records to satisfy the C.E.O, the Artist can get anything he wants. But, as soon as your record sales drop, you may as well get prepared to be treated just like your sales and get dropped. This is why it is important to take your life and career into your hands and be more self-sufficient and independent.

I was looking for my big break for over 20 years and that break never came. Well, I can't say it never came because I was presented with many great opportunities that could have turned into something great and let's just say that I let a lot of good opportunities pass me by. But everything happens for a reason, whether good or bad. The way I see it, when someone makes it big and becomes rich and famous, it's not because their break came, it's because it was destined to happen. See, when Nelly blew up, it was because Nelly was born to be who he is. When Martin Luther King, Jr. was born, he was born to be the great leader of the Civil Rights Movement.

Michael Jordan was born to be the greatest basketball player ever. So what I am trying to convey is, if it was meant for my alter ego, (Dr. Ease), to be rich and famous…through destiny it would have happened no matter what situation I was in, no matter what record exec I was dealing with or to what record label I was signed. There is one thing a person cannot stop, and that's destiny. Indulge me while I dig a little deeper. I believe that everyone's life is already written. Everything from what you will become in life to the date you will die. When your time comes, whether it is stardom or death, it is something that cannot be stopped.

A lot of you may disagree with me, and that's fine. But it's my book and my personal opinion. I went from Artist to Record Company Executive and now a writer. And who knows if any of my books will ever "blow-up?" It was destined for me to be a writer, to share my thoughts and experiences with the world.

Fresh Force

My first group was called Fresh Force. There were four of us; Gerald Williams, (Beat Master-Gee), Mike Wallace, (Cool-Ice), Mel Shaun Everett (DJ Cut-Wiz), and myself, Darryl Easley, (Dr.Ease).

One day, a friend of mine called me and told me that I had to hear this guy from Trotwood Madison High School Beat Box. (For those of you who are not familiar with the term "Beat Box", that is when someone makes drum beat sounds with their mouth like Dougie Fresh or Buffy from the Fat Boys.) This guy started making all these incredible sounds with his mouth that just blew me away. I arranged for the two of us to meet the following weekend. Once Gerald and I met, we became the best of friends.

I attended Meadowdale High School. That's where I met Mike Wallace. We both played football and we used to Rap against each other at practice or in the lunchroom back in 1983. Back in the days, a guy named Mark Jones, (The Hustler), used to throw high school parties around town. We heard that the Hustler was hosting a big Rap contest at the Lakeview Palladium. So, Gerald, Mike and I, along with a guy named Stan Grimes, (Rappin Stan) all decided to join forces and try to win the $200 prize money. We all met at my mother's house and came up with the name "Fresh Force". Back in 1983, the word "fresh" was the thing to say when you thought something was "hot". "Force" came from all of us joining forces to become one group. When we arrived at the Palladium, we were all pretty much cool and confident.

Well, everyone but Stan. He was nervous as hell. Every time I looked at him, he was shaking so hard he made me nervous. When it was time for us to hit the stage, there were only two microphones and there were four of us. We decided to give Gerald a Mic because he made the beats with his mouth, while the rest of us shared the other mic. On the intro, we all grabbed the microphone and Stan was shaking like buttcheeks. I tried to pull the microphone away from him and his grip was so tight that as I pulled, it snapped up and popped me right in the mouth…in front of everyone.

I felt better after we shared the 200 bones we took home for winning the contest. A few weeks later, a new guy named Melshunn Everett came to our school from Cleveland, Ohio. Melshunn was a DJ and a very brilliant person. He could hook his turn tables up to anything and get the party started. Once we hooked up…it was a wrap. Fresh Force won every contest we participated in. After we had been together for a while as a group, we decided to talk to Gerald's Uncle Sonny who had a nice pre-production studio on Grand Avenue. Sonny was a writer for The Ohio Players. He wrote the song "Sight for Sore Eyes" for them. He also had three top producers on his team; Reggie Morgan, Ronald Nooks and Billy Beck. Ronald and Billy played for the Ohio Players at the time.

The producers would lay down some tracks, (music), and we would choose which ones we liked and wanted to write our lyrics to and develop concepts for the songs. Sonny taught us how to count beats and bars and how to put a song together. Sonny was very instrumental in developing our talent as writers. After recording three good songs for our demo, Sonny promised the group that we would have a single out by summer.

We all told our families and friends that our single would be in stores in a matter of months. Everywhere we went, someone would ask us when our single would be released. We would say, "In the summer". Summer came and went… no single. After winning a few more talent shows, the Fresh Force was a household name in Dayton. We started having "fans". We would tour the recreational parks throughout the city and we had a big following. Other groups that where hot at the time were: Icy Hot, The Incomparable Force, The First Family and CJ Snow. We all got along with one another but we battled it out in the parks and at high school games at half time. A big show came up at Roosevelt Center with Channel 7 News covering the event. They interviewed us and shot a film of our performance. We tore the roof off that night but we lost to a female Rap group, Gwen Blackstone and 4 of her friends. After we were on the news that night, we really became Ghetto Superstars. We had plenty of female fans and we loved it.

Gerald and I became very close friends. Whenever you saw one of us, you saw the other. His Mom became our first manager. She ensured that when we got paid for a performance that we didn't get shorted.

The group started to sour after Sonny took Gerald out of my group and put him with another group of guys that started coming to his studio. The name of the group was 3-D and the group consisted of Derrick Hall (Devil D) and Derrick Smith (Master D). Derrick Hall was the leader of the group and he wrote a song called Jason, about the Friday the 13th movie character. The song was really good…actually, it was a great song. Derrick was and still is the greatest writer I have ever met in my life. Derrick introduced me to a guy named Russell Pryor who also rapped and beat boxed. From the beginning,

Russell and I clicked and became good friends. Before the group split, we performed at a fundraiser for Channel 45 which was held at the Dayton Convention Center. After our performance, an executive from the station said that he was very impressed with our performance. He asked if we would be interested in doing a commercial on Martin Luther King Jr. for Black History Month. Of course, we all agreed and the next weekend, we were at the television studio excited to be recording a commercial. The commercial aired the entire month of February, 1984. It sometimes aired 3 or 4 times a day. By this time, I was a junior in high school and I can remember feeling so good about myself and this "Rap" thing. I felt that I had finally accomplished something. After the commercial aired, we went up a notch in our Ghetto superstardom. We signed autographs wherever we went and someone always noticed us. Looking back, this was my first real taste of fame.

Unique Cut; My First Contract

It was 1986 and Russell and I decided to form a group called Unique Cut. We came together after a concert we opened for L.L. Cool J at Central State University's May weekend celebration. Russell was the beat box while Devil D and I were the Rappers. During our performance, our sound kept fading in and out. After this happened several times, I guess Devil D couldn't take it anymore and he just left the stage.

Russell and I stayed and I told the crowd that we didn't need any music and I motioned for Russell to start beat boxing. When he started…I started Rapping to his beat and the crowd went nuts. After that, it was Unique Cut all the way.

After we left the stage, we were approached by a man that told us he really enjoyed our showmanship and that he knew a guy in Columbus, Ohio that was looking for a Rap group.

ALMOST THERE

About a week later, Russell and I were in Columbus meeting with the CEO of Mainway Records, Mr. William "Pablo" Davis. He listened to our demo and then said he wanted us to join his roster of talent, which included: Midnight Star and The Deele.

Those two names alone made us want to sign the contract right on the spot. Midnight Star and the Deele had hit songs on the radio and at that time they were major acts. They both recorded in a studio called Bison Studios. Pablo gave us a tour of the studio and introduced us to the members of the groups. One of the members of The Deele would produce us. After we left the studio, Pablo gave us contracts to look over, sign and return the following weekend. Russell and I enlisted a guy named Rashad to be our DJ. Rashad was working at a local night club called Gambles. He would call me to the DJ booth and I would perform a song called "Go Dr. Ease" to the EPMD song "You Gots to Chill" while Rashad would be cutting it up. The crowd would love it. We also enlisted the help of Rachelle Ramey and Vern Wheeler as management.

Russell and I went back the following weekend and in front of our mothers, we signed the contract. A week later, we were back in the studio waiting to find out which member of The Decle would produce us. As we sat in the lobby of Bison Studio, The Deele came out to the lobby to take a break. Pablo introduced us to Stanley Burke(Stick). Stick was from Dayton, so Pablo felt that he would be the best person to work with us because we came from the same hometown. After the introduction, we went into the studio to watch The Deele record. Then Stick took us into Studio B and laid down a funky drum track. added some keys to it and told us to write to that song and bring it back completed next week. Everything was like clockwork. We would watch The Deele record and then go to Studio B with Stick to record. After watching them record so much, I noticed two guys that stood out the most with writing and producing. Their names were L.A. and Babyface. To make a long story short…about three months after we signed to the label, Midnight Star and The Deele had some sort of falling-out with Pablo and they parted ways. That pretty much closed the doors to Main Way Records.

After the split, two members started to write and produce for acts like the Whispers, and became one of the most sought after production duo in the industry. L.A. and Babyface went on to start LA Face Records. They signed acts such as Outkast, Toni Braxton, TLC and many others. Currently, L.A. runs Island Def Jam and TLC sold 10 million records and became the highest selling female group of all time. Outkast is still selling Mega records. Imagine for a moment what could have happened if Pablo had chosen LA or Babyface to produce us instead of Stick. We would have had an established relationship with LA Face and it wouldn't have been a problem for me to pick up the phone and call one of them for a record deal. In this business, 95 percent of the people that get signed are because someone knew somebody. I look back on

ALMOST THERE

that situation, the places I've been and the people I met and I realize that you never know that the person standing right next to you would someday blow-up and be a famous person. I then realized that when dealing with the music industry, it's not always what you know, but who you know. And my encounter with Mainway Records was another opportunity that was pulled away from me and once again...I was *Almost There*……..

THE BIG MOVE TO CALI

Russell, Rashad and I had a concert at Gambles, a local night spot in our hometown. Russell's Uncle, Alan, was home visiting from San Diego. Alan came to the show and was amazed at how good our performance was. After the show, he said that we could make a lot of money in California with the "hook-ups" he had. He said that he was a concert promoter and that he managed two bands. He also told us that he had a small independent label called Alan Magic Lamp Records.

The next day, he talked to all of our parents and assured them that if we came to San Diego, we would have jobs at UPS making $9.00 an hour. And he would book concerts for us every weekend and we would make anywhere from $600 to $1,200 per show. All we had to do was get to Cali. So Russell, Rashad and I scraped up bus fair and caught the Greyhound bus to California. The bus ride took three days but with three of us travelling together, it was really fun. All we did was dream and fantasize about making it big, moving to Hollywood and sending for family members to come and enjoy life in Cali with all the stars. When we arrived in Cali, Alan and a friend of his Lavell were there to welcome us. We loaded up the pick-up truck and hopped in the back. As we rolled through town, we saw two of the finest women with big boobs and nice legs. Rashad and I started screaming at them from the back of the truck. Alan and Lavell started laughing at us. Alan said, "Those two fine ass women you all were looking at were two fine ass men. They're called transvestites". Needless to say, Rashad and I were quiet the rest of the way to Alan's house.

Once we arrived at Alan's, we did not receive a warm welcome from his wife Ronnie. She told us from the jump, "You are on your own. Don't ask me to do anything for you because I'm against you coming into my home. I won't cook or clean after you." They had a three-bedroom apartment. Alan and his wife had one room, their two kids in another while Russell, Rashad and I stayed in the third room. Three men, one bed and three suitcases. We took turns sleeping in the twin sized bed. The other two had the floor. It was a very uncomfortable situation from the start.

Now, keep in mind that it was 1987 and the Crips and Bloods were at war. The first two days we were there, two kids and a pregnant woman were killed by stray bullets from gang activity. The neighborhood we stayed in was Blood territory. So, we couldn't wear blue. I remember getting dressed one morning, getting ready to go outside and Alan said, "man…you can't wear that outside. You can't wear blue in this neighborhood." Now, my favorite color is blue, so basically everything I brought to Cali had blue in it. I had two choices: 1) go outside and get my ass shot off by a Blood, or 2) go shopping and get a few outfits with neutral colors in them. Needless to say, I picked choice #2. I bought three short outfits with the little money I had left. I knew in a few days we would be getting paid for the show that was scheduled for the following Saturday.

Saturday rolled around and we opened for Alan's Bands, Joker and Mask. After the show, we asked Alan if we could get paid for our performance and he said he paid his groups on Monday because he was paid by check not cash. At this point, I'm broke, Rashad is broke and Russell is broke, because we had all depended on getting our $600 for our performance that night. Sunday, I asked Alan about our Jobs at UPS. He said he would take us in the morning. Monday morning, we all got dressed and went down to UPS. Alan stayed in the car while Russell, Rashad and I went inside to ask for applications. We were told that they were not hiring at that time. When we got back to the car,

Alan asked us, "What did they say"? We told him that they were not hiring and he said, "Okay, let's go." Now remember, he told us that the jobs were guaranteed for us when we got to Cali. That was one reason my Mom let me go… so that we could get jobs and move out on our own and not continue living with Alan and his family. My mom also told me to give Alan money for the food we ate while staying at his home once we got paid for doing the show.

I asked Alan when we were going to get paid for the show and he just said, "I want ya'll to ride with me to go pick up Ronnie from work." When we arrived at her job, she got into the car and asked Alan if he had told us yet. Alan said, "No." then Ronnie said, "The money you all made at the show, we are using to put food back into the refrigerator. Now I'm pissed, I'm broke and I said, "We didn't eat $600 worth of food." She said that we didn't make $600; we made $10 per song.

We did three songs so we made $30 for our performance. Now we are 3,000 miles away from home, broke and fucked-up, and this woman is telling me that we got $30 for our performance. When we arrived at Alan's house, Russell, Rashad and I had a group meeting outside. I told Russell, "Your uncle is fucking us." He said his uncle wasn't that kind of guy and he wouldn't do that. We agreed to tough it out and hang in there to see what happens next. When I woke up on Tuesday, I went into the kitchen to get some water. I sat at the table and noticed a check for $600 written out in our group's name, "*Unique Cut*". I told the fellas and they said, "talk to Alan when he comes home" as if I was the fucking spokesperson for the group.

When Alan came home, I asked him if we could talk. We sat down and I told him that I had seen the check on the table made out to our group. He responded with, "I told the promoter to put it in your group's name, but the money is for the Bands. What could I say? (That's bullshit, you lying fuck). I wanted to say that but I was 3000 miles away from home, with no money and nowhere to go. The next show came on Wednesday at a local swap-meet.

A swap-meet is a big warehouse full of different booths set-up to sell things like jewelry, shoes, clothes, records and even nail salons. Almost anything you could want was at the swap-meet. We performed outside and during our show; Russell and I would call each other Cuz. We were such good friends that we told people we were cousins. Every time we said "what's up Cuz", a guy kept on pulling up his shirt, showing us his pistol that was tucked inside his waistband. After the show, the guy came over to us and said, "you all were about to get shot on stage." We asked why and he said because we were in blood territory and we kept saying "Cuz".

Cuz means Crip, so we were disrespecting his hood. Then he said the only reason he let us all live was because we said that we were from Ohio when we were on stage. Then he said, "So don't let it happen again!" As the Blood walked off, one of the security guards from the Swap-meet approached us and asked if everything was alright.

He complemented us on our performance and said he rhymed a little and that he was from Chicago. His name was Tony Seals. Tony and I swapped phone numbers, chatted for a while and found that we had a lot in common. So, he invited me to come to a party that his boy Derek was giving that night. Later that night, Tony came by and picked me up and we hung out all night just kickinit.

Tony and I became really close friends. He even hooked me up with a job as a security guard at the Swap Meet. I told him we came all this way from Ohio to get screwed around and I had no money to get home. He pulled some strings and got me in. Tony even picked me up and took me to work and when he got off before me, he would come all the way back from his home to take me home when I got off. Tony schooled me on Cali-Life. He took me everywhere and showed me the real Cali. He even hooked me up with his girlfriend's sister. I ate dinner at his home with him and his girlfriend all the time. If it wasn't for Tony and his girl taking me in, I would have gone home 100 pounds lighter than when I left… from starvation. The funny thing is that his girl couldn't really cook that well. And he warned me of this the first time he invited me over for dinner, but Dammit, when you're hungry… a cracker tastes like a steak, so I wasn't going to complain.

Back to the job at the Swap Meet…the only thing I didn't like was that it was always an altercation between like 5 Crips and 5 Bloods and we would have to get in between the feud. Needless to say, I didn't like that, because after you broke them up, they would always threaten to come back and get you. But overall, it was a job and a way for me to get back home…soon. The other thing I didn't like was the Swap Meet closed at 8:00 pm and sometimes, I would be scheduled to work until 11:00 pm. So, I had to sit outside in front of the store and patrol the building every 30 minutes. If I had a car, I could have sat in my car, but since I didn't, I had to sit by the pay phones in front, next to a bench.

Faces of Death

Many times I would hear gunshots from gang activity going on. I worked there for about two months. My last day of work came when I was doing that outside late shift and a car pulled into the Swap Meet parking lot. It was a white Cadillac with a blue ragtop and the car approached me real slow. As the car stopped a few feet away, I could see it was a car full of Crips. They looked at me, smiled and pulled-off into the night. Now keep in mind, the store was in Blood territory, so I had a bad feeling that something was about to go down.

    I started thinking back on some of those gang fights that I had broken-up in the store and Crip threats that came my way. A few minutes later, I looked across the parking lot and saw two guys coming my way. They both had on white T-shirts, blue jeans saggin and blue bandanas around their heads with Locs on. (Locs are dark shades). It's about 10:30 PM and they had on dark glasses. Now being in the position that I was in; no gun - no car, (I didn't even have a rock to chuck at them), my survival instincts kicked-in and I had to think fast.

    All I had was a walkie talkie to call my supervisor in case something happened. By the time I called him and he arrived to help me, I would have been shaking hands with Jesus. The guys coming at me were about 5'5" or 5'6". I was 6'2" and 240 at the time. I had to think quick, so I grabbed the pay phone and started talking. No one was on the other end. I just wanted them to get close enough to grab one of them and at least, fight for my life if they pulled-out guns. So I'm having a conversation with the dial tone and once they got a few feet away, they stopped. I told the dial tone to hold on, and asked the Crips if I could help them. Then, one of them said, "Have you seen a bitch?" I said no, and got back on the phone, at the same time praying for my life because they weren't close enough for me to make my move on them. So I said to the dial tone, "yo, you almost here?

You're right around the corner? Okay, I'm ready." I hung up the phone right when the operator said, *"If you'd like to make a call, please hang up......"* I'm not sure if they heard the beeping that comes in when the phone is off the hook, because they just stood there looking at me. So, I tried to be hard and said in a strong deep voice… "what, you didn't hear me? I said I didn't see no bitch." When in all actuality I was saying, "please don't shoot me! Let me walk away with my life."

Then, (Pow Pow), two gun shots went off up the street, the white Cadi drove up fast into the parking lot. The driver said, "Get the fuck in and let's ride …leave him." The two Crips smiled at me and one pulled out a pistol…pointed it at me and said, "It must be your lucky day because you where that bitch I was looking for." They hopped in the car and drove off. I stood there for a minute. I could actually feel my heart about to burst through my chest. My hands started to shake really bad and I saw my mother and kids flash before my eyes. My stomach began to hurt and I almost shit on myself. I realized that death was standing right in front of me.

A tear rolled down my cheek…then my heartbeat slowed, my hands stopped shaking and I felt a calmness come over my body. Maybe God pulled the devil off of my shoulder. I got myself together, called Frank on the walkie talkie and told him he could come and get his uniform and his walkie talkie…they both would be on the bench next to the payphone. I would have walked home bucket-naked if I stayed another minute. Tony pulled up and gave me a ride home.

That was my first experience with death and I want to thank God for allowing me to live through that experience, because if I wasn't about to die right there in that parking lot…then I was *almost there.*

Shake Down

One night, Tony, Russell, Rashad and I were playing basketball at the apartment complex and the manager of the complex yelled out his window that it was too late to play basketball and to go home. We would give the guy a hard time. One morning, I was getting ready for work and went into the bathroom, and while I was washing up, I heard all these police sirens and fire trucks. I figured damn… something was really going on. I heard some walkie talkies right under my window, so I figured I would take a look outside to see what was going on. To my surprise, as soon as I peeped out I locked eye contact with a member of the S.W.A.T team.

He ducked behind a car and said, "He's up there…I just saw him look out."

At this time, I'm scratch' n my head, so I take another look and sure enough the S.W.A.T team ducked behind some cars and yelled for me to come out with my hands up, NOW! I pulled my head away from the window so fast, I almost gave myself whiplash. I woke Ronnie and Rashad and we all went to the front door. As I opened the door, I saw that the police were everywhere. They instructed us to come down one-by-one with our hands where they could see them. I went first with my hands in the air as instructed. As I walk slowly down the stairs with guns pointed at me from all directions, I'm saying to myself, "what is going on now."

When I reached the last step, a police officer pulled me off the last step, threw me to the ground and put his gun to the back of my head. I asked the officer what the problem was and he told me to [shut the fuck up] and be still. One-by-one, everyone exited the apartment and was thrown to the ground. Now everyone who lived in the complex was outside watching and wondering what was going down. After everyone was out of the house, one officer came over and said that a 7-11 store was robbed and the complex manager said that he saw someone run into our apartment with a gun. They told us that the store employee was on his way in a police car to identify the suspect. Now at this point, I'm scared to death. I'm thinking… "what if this witness is white?"

Because they think all black folk look alike anyway, he might come over here and pick me as the shooter in the robbery. The cruiser pulls up and an officer grabs my arm and leads me out to the middle of the street, and out of his walkie talkie I heard, "suspect turn to your right." So I did. Then I heard, "turn to your left." So I did, and after about 30 seconds, I heard an officer say, "Negative." They take Rashad and do him the same way, and after his inspection they said negative again.

Then, after all of that, they told us that they were sorry for the inconvenience and left like nothing ever happened. Like they never violated us and embarrassed us in front of everyone. Thinking back on that day in Cali, I'm glad that I didn't go to jail on a robbery charge. But then again, when I think back on that day, what bothers me most is, if that cashier wanted to send a black man to jail that day, whether they committed the crime or not, then I was *almost there*....

That day was the breaking point for me. I knew I had to swallow my pride and call home before something happened to me. Maybe GOD was trying to tell me to get out of Cali. So I called home and told my mother what had happened and she called my grandmother, Mrs. Geraldine Smith and told her I needed to get home. My grandmother sent me bus fare a couple of days later and it was a done deal. That weekend, DR. EASE was going back home to Dayton, Ohio. Honestly, I should have done that a month earlier, but my pride wouldn't let me. I felt that if I came home with nothing that I was a complete failure, and a fool for even going that far on someone's word, someone that turned out to be full of hot air. We all took a trip to Tijuana the day before I left. Tijuana is right across the border from San Diego. As we were going into Tijuana, you could see illegal immigrants trying to sneak over. The ones that got caught were beaten all the way back over the border. Once we got into Tijuana, the city smelled just like urine, and you could see an entire family sleep on the ground with bath towels covering them for blankets. Little girls aged 12 and 13 years with make-up on trying to look older prostituting themselves for money and yet, everyone from Diego went over there to party almost every weekend. This didn't feel right to me.

As we walked down the strip, they had plenty of strip clubs. We checked out a few and ended up in a hip-hop club on the 3rd floor of some building. My boys and I kicked it until six in the morning. Just when we were about to leave, a group of guys came into the club and gave the D.J. a 12-inch record to play. When he played the record, I was trippin out, because the record had all kind of cursing in it, talking about hookers and calling women bitches and hoes, getting blow jobs and saying things like "fuck the police." As one of the group members walked past me, the back of his jacket read N.W.A. They were there promoting the album by Eazy-E called EAZY DUZ IT. The song was called BOYS IN THE HOOD. The whole time we were there, Russell and Rashad tried talking me out of leaving. I told Russell that he was there with his family and that he was comfortable but I was not comfortable living the way we were living and being treated the way we were being treated. My mind was made up; I was outta there in the morning. I was 18 years old and I felt that if I stayed another week, I probably would have not made it to be 19. So I swallowed my pride and took my black ass home.

    The next morning came before I knew it. The bus was scheduled to leave at 8 o'clock. I did not sleep because we were out until 6 in the morning. I had nothing to pack because I was living out of my suit case in the first place. Rashad and I talked for a few, while I counted my money right in front of him. I had $103 dollars left from my last check from the swap meet. I put it in my wallet, went to the rest room, came back, said my good byes and bounced. Tony came to take me to the bus station. On the way, I expressed my appreciation for everything that he had done for me. I told him that I would never forget him and if I ever blew up, that I would look out for him just like he did for me. Once at the station, we gave each other a hug and a pound and he left. In all honesty, Tony Seals' friendship was about the only thing I missed about San Diego.

LONG RIDE HOME

Once I boarded the Greyhound, I had to get myself mentally prepared for this long ass ride home. It was different on the way to Cali, because I had two close friends rollin' with me, but on the way back, I was rollin' solo. After the first 3 hours, the bus pulled over at a rest stop, I wasn't hungry so I stayed on the bus.

I was recuperating from the long night I spent in Tijuana. I must have slept a good 4 hours because the next time I woke, we were in New Mexico. I was thirsty so I grabbed my wallet and got an instant migraine headache, because when I opened my wallet, all I saw was 3 one-dollar bills. I looked all through my wallet and that $100 dollar bill was nowhere to be found. So I pulled out one dollar, put it into the pop machine and pushed the Pepsi button…no pop came out. So trying to be smart, I thought that if I put another dollar in the machine, I would get 2 pops; one for now, and one for later. So I put another dollar in the machine but this time, I pushed Mountain Dew, and once again, no pop. It took everything in my heart not to cry.

All I could think about was that I had 3 more days on that bus with one-dollar left. Needless to say, I lost all control, I started kicking and cursing the machine out, I even took off my belt and started whup'n the machine like it stole something. Actually it did…my 2 fucking dollars. Now I'm sitting on the bus, my mouth dry as hell, and I'm tired from kicking that machine's ass. On top of all of that, it seemed that the bus driver was pulling over every 5 freak'in minutes at some food joint to get something to eat. And every time he stopped, he looked right at me and smiled before he hollered out "food-stop!"

I couldn't even buy one slice of pizza, so I grabbed a bag of potato chips that was 99 cents and went to the counter. I actually prayed that I wouldn't have to pay taxes on them. If I did, I probably would have run out the pizza place with them, jumped on the bus and ate as many chips as I could before the police arrived. If you ever saw the movie Jo-Jo dancer about Richard Pryor's life, the part when he was on the bus and his stomach was growling because he was so hungry… that was me. All I could do was try sleeping so as to keep my mind off of food. But even when I went to sleep, I would dream about eating a big ass cheeseburger.

The second day of the bus ride, we pulled into some hick town at a food joint. So I got off the bus to go use the restroom, and when I walked through the door, all I could smell was some good ole fried chicken. As I searched around for the restrooms, I noticed that they were a few feet away from the food line. So I grabbed a food tray and stood in line like I had $300 dollars to spend on food. At the end of the line, they had fruit and down closer to the cashier, they had the meat, so I grabbed an apple, orange and a juice, and when the cashier turned her head, I dipped around the corner to the restroom. Once inside, I put a smashing on the apple and put the orange in my pocket. As I exited out of the restroom, I thought to myself that I was going to go to jail over some fruit. But that was a chance that I had to take. I was nervous as hell, but I was chewing my ass off at the same time, in case someone saw me.

I didn't want to leave any evidence. I know you all are laughing at me, but damn that… I had a day and a half left on that bus and I was losing weight in record time. When I left Diego, I was 240 pounds and after a day and a half, I was 200 pounds. It's not good to lose 40 pounds in a day. I was a hongry M…F…Yes I said HONGRY; let me explain the difference. When you eat breakfast Monday morning and then lunch Monday evening in-between, you may have been hungry. When you eat breakfast Monday morning and you don't eat again until Wednesday evening, then your ass is HONGRY! I swear I saw a thousand promotional signs for Burger King, Wendy's and McDonalds with big ass whoppers and Big Macs and double cheeseburgers on them. I could smell the food coming right off the signs. I swear it made me want to jump off the bus, run up one of those signs and bite the shit out of one.

On a serious tip, it wasn't funny at the time. I wanted to catch another bus back to Cali, and whup Rashads ass and then catch another one back home. But things happen for a reason and he needed it more than I did. If he had asked me, I would have given him half of what I had, but you learn and move on. Rashad, if you are reading this book, I just want to say that

    I FORGIVE YOU…

Put Your Mind & Body At Ease "89"

Ease Town Posse

THE RISE AND FALL OF BULLSEYE RECORDS

After being back home for about a week, my friend, Robert Henderson hooked me up with a job at a casting company called Advanced Foundry making ten dollars an hour. I considered myself finished with the music industry. One Saturday, Bert and I went to Gambles night club and I saw Robert Moore. Rob was part of a promotional company called Bullseye Production. He asked me how Cali was and told me they were promoting a concert the following month with N.W.A. and Chubb Rock and asked if I would be interested in opening the show. We exchanged phone numbers and hooked up the next day. Rob and I called each other cousins because I had two daughters by his cousin Terri. I agreed to let him manage me and see what would happen.

Bullseye Production was made up of a few Ballers, not basketball players either, (If you know what I mean). The president of the company's name was Herk and the vice president's name was 2-Pot. Then you have Rob and Buster (John Lewis) that helped out and played different roles like Road Manager, etc. Bullseye Productions had just rented a building on Gettysburg Ave next to Nicholi's IGA. They had four office spaces and the back was like a rehearsal hall. Big Rob would allow my group and I to practice in the rehearsal spot. The N.W.A. show was on a Saturday night. The group flew in on Friday Morning. My group and I were rehearsing in the hall when all of a sudden, the door flung open and there they were; Ice Cube, Dr. Dre, DJ Yella, Eazy E, MC Ren, LA Law and another guy who I had never heard of before. We automatically stopped rehearsing. Dr. Dre came up and introduced himself to me and the others followed, one-by-one, shaking my hand and introducing themselves to our group. Eazy E said, "Go ahead and finish as if we're not here."

So, I gave the que to my DJ who at the time was DJ Mix, (Ben Clay). Ben was a world-class sprinter for Central State University. We went through our show and the group gave us props and asked if we had a mall close around. So, we all loaded up the van and took them to the Salem Mall, hung out and kicked it with them. Dr. Dre and Eazy E hung out with me and DJ Mix. Ice Cube and MC Ren kicked it with 2-Pot. On the way back to the hotel, I asked the guy I never heard of what his name was and he told me D.O.C. and went on to tell me he was from Texas and that Dr. Dre was going to produce him after N.W.A's album was complete.

And sure enough, three years later, the D.O.C. was one of my favorite rappers with a hot single called "It's Funky Enough." Saturday came and both groups were at Hara Arena. Chubb Rock and N.W.A. did their sound check and then we went behind them and did ours. When we were done, we all went back stage and kicked it. I told them that I remembered seeing them in Tijuana promoting Boys-N-the Hood. Before we knew it, it was almost show time and we got dressed for the show. Before we went on, N.W.A. told us to "have a good show." At the beginning of our show, our intro beat came on and my dancers; Nite & Day came on stage dancing. When it was time for DJ Mix to hit the stage, that was exactly what he did.

He tripped on the side of the stage and tried to keep his balance but stumbled all the way to the turn tables where he fell on the floor right behind them. To play it off, DJ Mix reached his hand up and started scratching while his body was on the floor. The crowd lost it and went nuts. I guess they figured it was part of the show. When I hit the stage, the crowd was already heated and ready for my flow. We gave a great performance and our home town crowd was with us all the way to the end. Chubb Rock came on after us and gave a good performance, when N.W.A. hit it, it was all over. They were rock' in cuts like, "Boyz-N-the Hood", 8 Ball and Dope Man. For about 45 minutes, N.W.A. rocked the crowd. We left the concert and took N.W.A. to a nightclub called Gambles where 2-Pot got Ice Cube drunk as hell; and a few women to go along with his drinks. Eazy-E partied 'till 3 am and the next morning, 2-Pot took them to the airport and they flew to the next city on their tour. I am very proud to say that I had the pleasure of meeting and hanging out with Eazy-E before he died of AIDS in 1995. A guy named Ron Patterson was at the N.W.A. show. Ron lived in Atlanta and worked for a record label called Itchiban, which was the number one independent distributor in the world. Ron told Herk that he should start a record label and sign me as his first act. He told Herk that he could talk to John Abbey, the owner of Itchiban about distributing Bullseye Records. Herk asked me how much would it take to record an album. I gave him a few quotes on what studio time cost by the hour and he told me that he and 2-Pot would pay for my recordings and that I would sign a contract with their label. I agreed and put my group together. Nite & Day, stayed on as my dancers, Broderick Dumas and Vincent Ward. Robert Henderson was my hype man (Magnum) and Lamar Moody became DJ Mix after Ben Clay had to commit all of his time to running track in which he had a full scholarship. The Ease-Town Posse was born featuring Dr.Ease. We ended up recording at ReFraze Studio in Kettering, Ohio…a million dollar spot. I got busy writing and producing the whole album with help from DJ Mix on the production end. At the end of all the hard work and hours we put in, we came up with my first album. It was called, "Put Your Mind and Body at Ease." Herk and 2-Pot paid for the recording and we shipped the material to Ron Patterson in Atlanta. A week later, we drove to Atlanta to sign the distribution deal. After everything was sealed, we took pictures for the album cover. I chose to go to the Dayton Art Institute because it had a very nice background and it's a symbolic place for Dayton, Ohio. 2-Pot brought his white Corvette drop-top and for the back of the album cover, the Ease-Town Posse gathered around the car for a photo.

    About a month later, Herk called and said the album cover was done and we could come and get our copies. I remember being so damn excited that I was finally about to see myself on an album cover. So actually one of my dreams did come true, the day Herk handed me my first ever album with my picture on the front of it. My dream also came true when my album was being sold in stores across the nation, right next to other artists that I admired like; LL Cool J, Public Enemy, Whodini and many others. Maybe I should have Dreamed of being rich off the sales of the album also, instead of just having my face on the cover. If that was the case, then my dream came true 5 times because I have 4 full lengths CD's and 1 single with my face plastered on the front cover.

When my album was released in 1989, I think I went to every record store in the city just to see it on the shelves. I was high for about 2 weeks straight. Not high on drugs, but high on life and the feeling of knowing that I accomplished something positive with my life. Something my family was proud of. It felt good that every time I went somewhere that someone would come up to me and let me know that they have my album at home. You may have 100 other rappers come out of Dayton, but I was the first to come out of Dayton on a National level. So, that makes me a Dayton Hip-Hop Pioneer. Just like Kurtis Blow was the first rapper to have a certified gold single, that's something you can never take from me. The first to do anything is a great accomplishment in itself.

Ron told us about Jack the Rapper. It was a big event in Atlanta given by a guy named Jack Gibson, one of the first Black radio personalities. It was an annual event where any and everyone in the music business would come to Atlanta to network, party and kick it. It was an all weekend affair that took place at the Marriott Hotel close to the airport. Friday night was for new talents to perform and hopefully gain the interest of a major label. Saturday was a celebrity basketball game, swim parties and "labels" threw parties on every floor of the 20-storey hotel. I remember going to the 5th floor to the DefJam sponsored party, then going to the 10th floor to the Capitol Records party and then to the 20th floor where Motown had their party. Every floor was off–the-hook! On Friday, my group performed, and we gave one hell of a show. On Saturday, at the Celebrity ball game, M.C. Hammer called my name from the stands and showed me a picture of our group in a magazine called B.R.E (Black Radio Exclusive).

The article raved about our performance. I was on cloud 9 because this was once again, a dream come true. For me to be in a national magazine such as B.R.E., a magazine that is sent to every Black radio station in the nation was another great feat for Dr. Ease & the Ease Town Posse; and for Bullseye Records. After our performance on Friday, Heavy D and Dougie Fresh approached me and said, "you and your group gave one hell of a performance." I couldn't believe it. Someone like Dougie Fresh that calls himself the world's greatest entertainer gave me props on my show, and also Heavy D, who was a great performer himself. As soon as I walked off the stage, I was bombarded with cards from major record companies with connections to well-known independent labels as well. I had cards from Capitol Records, Warner Brothers Records, Def Jam, Rap-A-Lot, Loud Records and a host of other so-called important labels. All of them asked me to give them a call on Monday morning to discuss me coming to their label. But me being the loyal *MF* that I was, I gave every last card to my *so-called* Label Head, Herk, who in-turn never contacted any of the many labels that were courting me at Jack the Rapper. The head of Def Jam Records, Russell Simmons was one of the people that gave me his card and told me to call. He's like the Hip-Hop godfather. See, without Russell, there would be no Puffy, Master P, or Ruff Ryders or any black owned and operated record labels. What he went through was seen by these other rap moguls. Russell paved the way for those guys to be as successful as they are.

One thing I love about Russell Simmons is that he didn't compromise his love for Hip-Hop. He went into meetings with the major white heavy weights that wore suits and ties and he walked in straight Hip-Hop. He had his hat on backwards, jeans, no shoe strings in his shoes. See, the white heavy hitters probably underestimated his mind, because of the way he was dressed. But you can believe that when he left that meeting, all those guys saw was green…as in, how much money this guy can generate for their company. Rest assured that Russell got his right off the top. Russell was a huge opportunity I missed. Just consider all of the careers he jump started. One thing that makes upsets me now is the fact that I did not build relationships with all these huge owners and entertainers. Each and every card I received, I gave to my Manager who not once, called any one of them. I'm upset with myself for being loyal to a company that didn't have my best interest at heart.

All I became was a pawn in his game, so he could say, "I have a record company and this is my artist and this is how I was able to buy this Corvette, 750 BMW, $200,000 in jewelry and a $250,000 house with no fucking job." My word to up and coming Artists is, only show loyalty to those that show it to you. If there's no loyalty shown to you, then go for self. You see, I trusted other people to make the right choices concerning my career. That's the magic word…"my" career. Life is funny, a lot of times, you look back on somethings that happen in your life and wish you could have the opportunity to do it all over again.

But you can't change anything that has ever happened…it's in the past. That's why I say, take advantage of every opportunity that comes your way, because you won't be able to go back and grab that same opportunity that you let go by. Later on that night, which was Saturday, Luke Skywalker gave a party, (The Me so Horny Party), and showcased all of his groups, like: Poison Clan, 2 Live Crew and many others. When the 2 Live Crew came out on stage, they had twenty strippers walking around bucket naked. Men were having oral sex on them and everything. The hotel people raided the party and shut it down but those who had a chance to be there…got a hell of an eyeful.

I never saw so many stars in one place, in my life. It was awesome! In the main ballroom, Prince performed with his New Power Generation. In one incident, Eddie Murphy came in with like 10 guys around him and I remember watching other stars leave their chairs to go take a look at him. I know that had to make him feel so uncomfortable. Then, Jack got on the mic and told everyone to "sit their asses down, he's just another person."

My first time going to Jack-the-Rapper in Atlanta will be something that I will always remember. I followed that first trip with 5 more, and after my 5th time going, it was still exciting to go. One thing I have to say is that every time we went, something funny would always happen. One time, my group and I went to Jack-the-Rapper and after we checked into the hotel, everyone wanted to go swimming. So we all put on some swim trunks and went down to the pool. Everyone started jumping in and playing around. So when it was my turn, I dove in and right behind me, Brian (Bumble Bee) Ragsdale dove in next to me. He started bouncing up and down under the water playing like he was drowning, so I started laughing at him. After a few more times of him going under, I guess he heard me laughing because when he came up this time, he said, "help me motha fucka", with a mouth full of water. So I grabbed his arm and pulled him to safety. He immediately got out of the pool and got dressed. It was so funny; we tease him till this day. I always ask him, "Why did you jump in the deep end if you couldn't swim?" And he said he tried to jump deep enough to be able to stand up but he came up short.

Hammer Time

After returning from Jack the Rapper, a lot of things started happening real fast for me and Bullseye. The company promoted a concert at Hara Arena with major acts such as Public-Enemy, Too short, 3XDope, Special-Ed, Boogie Down Productions, and a guy no one ever heard of. I believe Ron asked Herk if he could add this guy to the show for a little of nothing and Herk agreed. It was also the first time I got to meet Chuck-D of Public Enemy…one of my favorite Rappers. His voice was so strong and I just knew he would be like 6'3" tall. When he walked past me, I thought to myself, he looks like Chuck-D.

When he turned around again, it was him…all 5'6" of him. At that time, Big Rob came up to me and said, "yo Ease, there's ya boy Chuck." We approached him and Rob introduced us. We shook hands and I told him how I was a fan of his music. I gave him a copy of my album and we talked a little more, he told me to have a good show and we went off to do sound check. After we opened the show, a guy named MC Hammer was introduced to the crowd. He came out dancing around and the crowd just kind of stared at him and his hype man, 2 Big MC. No one was really feeling Hammer. But, for some reason, Herk took a liking to him and his manager/brother, Louis. When Public Enemy hit the stage, it was chaos. The crowd went nuts. Public Enemy's show was so energetic and hype, it was ridiculous. One of the best shows I have ever seen in my whole life. Bullseye promoted another show the following month in Indianapolis, Indiana. The line-up was: Tony, Toni, Tone, Guy, MC Hammer, and Ease-Town Posse.

During the intermission, they played my single, "Make-U-Dance" over the speakers and MC Hammer asked Herk who that was and Herk told him it was me. Then Louis asked Herk who wrote the song and Herk told him that I did. Louis said that he wanted Hammer to do that song. Just like that and offered Herk $10,000 for the song. Just one month after never knowing anything about Hammer, he started blowing up! His songs, "Turn This Motha Out", and "They Put Me in The Mix" were released at the same time and were blowing up. That was the first time I saw two singles and two videos released at the same time. Hammer was now a household name.

At the show in Indiana, after we performed, Tony, Toni, Tone hit the stage, followed by Guy; Aaron Hall, Teddy Riley and Damon Hall. The show was great and Aaron Hall called himself Mr. Nasty Man. After seeing their show, I know why. During their performance Aaron grabbed a girl out of the audience and started singing to her. The female had on a mini skirt and after he sang to her for a while, he stopped and put his head under her skirt and started going to town. Or should I say, he went downtown to eat. After the show, I overheard her tell her friends that he really did that on stage. I felt like that was a bit much, but that was his choice. After Guy left the stage, MC Hammer came out and turned the motha out. Back stage, he kept asking Herk to sell him that song. Over the past few months, Herk, Louis and Hammer became close friends. When Hammer was just starting out,

 Herk kept on putting Hammer on the shows that Bullseye promoted, and Hammer told Herk if he made it big, he wouldn't forget the help Herk& Bullseye gave him. Needless to say, the next year, Hammer was a major super star selling like 20 million records worldwide with, "You Can't Touch This." At this time, Hammer is the biggest Rap star in the game and we had a personal relationship with this mega star. I remember Hammer had a show in Detroit at Joe Louis Arena and he called Herk and told him to bring his group down to hang out. We packed up two car loads and went to Detroit to kick it with him. Hammer left passes for all of us. He had a spot in his show where he would leave the stage and his bodyguards would make a circle in the middle of the floor and Hammer would dance. After Hammer got scratched by some crazy female fans, he would say go get the Ease-Town-Posse to help make the circle on the floor. It seemed that every time we would do a show with Hammer, he would ask us to help with the circle, we would joke around and say that we were gonna start charging him for our help because we would get scratched and bruised up because females were jumping on our backs just to touch him. Hammer would do three shows sometimes in one day, and I asked him, "how do you dance like that for three shows?"

He looked at me and said, "$100,000 a show". I guess for $300,000 a day, I would be a big Heavy-D moving, Funky Chicken swinging, Robot Dancing

"MF" too. I saw Hammer go from $5,000 a show to $100,000 a show, cartoons, commercial shoe endorsements in a very short period. We did a show in Jacksonville, Florida and then Mobile, Alabama and Flint, Michigan. When we came back to Dayton for a concert with Hammer and Public Enemy, Louis asked Herk how our record sales were. Herk told him it was moving, but not fast enough. Louis told Herk to shoot a video and after it aired on Rap City, we would sell like 50,000 units in no time and that was the new way of promoting your album. So Herk found someone to shoot our video. I wrote the script and the video crew and I got to work. We used a record store called Classic Records to shoot the Store signing scene. Thanks to Torrence McClendon who owned the store, and for the club scene we used Spunky's Night Club. Thanks to Ricky Poole who owned and operated Spunky's. Herk and 2-Pot pulled out the drop top corvettes, We had Marco and Michael Ecton who were DJ's on WDAO announce over the air that there will be a video shoot for the East-Town Posse and if you wanted to be in it…come down to the record store and Spunky's Night Club. We had a huge following and a lot of my Dayton People came to support me. It took hours to shoot and we kept doing the same scenes over and over and over. Overall, the video was decent.

Radio Promo Tour

Ichiban hooked Bullseye Records up with a lady named Charmaine. Her job was to take us out to Radio stations throughout the south. I was excited. It was my first radio promotional tour. Me, DJ Mix, big Rob and Charmaine headed south for my promo tour.

I always thought that if a radio station likes your record then they will play it… (Wrong). When we arrived at this certain Radio station, (I will not say any call letters because I may get sued), we did our interview on air, promoted our song and when we were done, Charmaine left with the PD. That's the program director, the person that decides whose record will be played on their station. When she came back, she told us that the Program Director said that if we give him one ounce of coke, he would play our record every hour on the hour. When I say coke, I ain't talking pop or soda kinda coke. I'm talking the coke with "aine" at the end of it.

So for one ounce of white stuff, we would have a hit in that city and surrounding areas. For one, I was offended, for two, how and where were we supposed to get this stuff? And if we did not get him what he wanted, he would not play our single. Well, we left without fulfilling his request.

ALMOST THERE

The second radio station was in another part of the south. We had our interview and a lot of callers called in and said that they were feeling my song. After we went off air, the PD said that if we got him a 5th of Jack Daniels, he would make my song a hit. Now that was something we could do. So, we marched down to the liquor store and got him not one…but two bottles of Jack Daniels and added a pint of Hennessy. Needless to say, our song was played every minute of the hour and reached #1 on that station and our record sales went up also.

One radio station and personality that basically played the song because he liked it, was a guy from Birmingham, Alabama who went by the name of "School Boy" at WENN 107.7. He pushed it so hard and he didn't ask for anything. Plus, he hooked us up with other shows in the area. We felt like we cheated him because he didn't want anything. So, we took him out to dinner when he got off the air. I would like to thank School Boy and WENN 107.7 for everything they did for me, my career and for making me #1 in Birmingham. After that, we asked the Program Directors if we could take them to dinner to show our appreciation for their help. We would ask them before they could ask us for anything that we didn't have or couldn't get. I'm going to keep it real with whoever reads this book. Whenever you hear a song on the radio that sounds like shit…it's because everything has a price, including Radio Stations…trust me.

DARRYL T. EASLEY

Ice-T

I first met Ice –T at a concert that we opened in Jacksonville, Florida in 1989. The shows acts were: Ice T, MC Lyte and the headliner was Kool Mo Dee. His album was hot at the time with hits like, "Wild Wild West" and "How you like me now". I didn't care much for Mo-D because he was stuck-up and every time I saw him, he never spoke. He just stared at me. I would speak and he never spoke back. Now Ice-T, while we were performing, stood on the side of the stage and watched our entire show. He was hyped, jump'in around and smiling.

After the show, he came to our dressing room, bragging on how good we were. We had a video camera 2-Pot brought with him to film our show and Ice-T said, "turn on that camera", and when 2-Pot hit "play", Ice-T started clowning around, talking about how good he thought we were and geeked us up. We exchanged phone numbers because that following week, we had another show together in Dayton, my hometown. He said he would call when he got into town and we could hang out together. Now, I'm thinking yeah, right… Ice-T wants to hang out with me. The following week, I came home from practice and my Mom said "some guy named Ice somebody called about 10 minutes ago; he said that he was at Stouffers Hotel downtown and wants you to come see him." Big Rob, DJ-Mix, my brother Kevin and I all went down to the hotel. When we arrived, it was crazy. About 200 women were in the lobby trying to get up to his room. His bodyguard told the women that he was sleeping and didn't want to be bothered. But as soon as he saw us walk in, he yelled out "Ease-Town-Posse come on up, Ice-T has been looking for yall." Everyone in the lobby looked at us like we were lucky to get in to see Ice-T. When we arrived at his door, he was sleeping, but when his DJ, Evil-E saw us, he let us in the room. Ice woke up and hugged everyone and said, "man, I called you and your Mom said you were gone." Thanks for coming by. Before you knew it, we had been in his room for 3 hours. He was schooling us on the whole Hip-Hop industry. He let us know who was real, who was fake and what to watch out for and what promoters to watch out for.

I told him that I appreciate a guy like him (who, to me, was considered to be a major player in the game at the time), taking time to sit me down and school me the way he did. He said that's just the kind of person he was and that if I looked out for him here in Dayton, that when we came to L.A., he would look out for us. He said he owned a club called Water the Bush in L.A., and that we could come anytime we wanted and perform. After our 3 1/2 hour talk, it was time to head to the show. We all rolled with Ice-T in their van and put on a great show. I respect Ice-T because he befriended me and he didn't have to. He schooled me on the game and told me the do's and don'ts of the business. I'm very happy to see his acting career do what it's doing. He deserves it.

The next show we did was in Mobile, Alabama and that

was probably the biggest show I've done with about 20,000 people. The show consisted of acts like, Heavy-D, 357, Hammer, Special Ed, Public Enemy and Ease-Town. When we first arrived into Mobile off of the highway, we pulled up to a stoplight and some guy was playing my single in his van. So, I rolled down the window and said "hey man, that song is jammin. Who is that?" And he said, "a new group called Ease-Town-Posse and they're gonna be at the concert tonight." So I said, "Are you going? "He said, "hell yeah, I've got to go see those cats live. After we checked into the hotel, a few of the workers asked for my autograph and they even went home to bring my album cover back to the hotel so I could sign it for them.

Later that day, we went to the mall and I felt like a real star because swarms of people kept coming up to me asking for autographs. Big Rob ended up being my body guard that whole day. You couldn't tell me shit. I was a rap superstar…finally. After the mall, we had a radio interview at the station and women kept calling in asking me if I wanted to have fun with them after the show. They wanted to know how old I was and if I wanted a Southern woman for the night. After we got off air, when we got ready to leave, there was like 50 women outside of the radio station waiting for us to come out. We had to get escorted out of the station to our van. After we entered the van and drove off, we had carloads of women following us and pulling up to our van flashing their breasts and smashing them up

ALMOST THERE

against the window.

Finally, it was show time. The promoter told us that we were the opening act, but since we have so many fans here and our song was #2 in Mobile, he was going to let us go on 3rd. So special-Ed went first, then 357, then Ease-Town. When we hit the stage, it was like magic. Everyone in the concert was singing my songs word for word and that was the best feeling in the world. After we left the stage, a female jumped down out of the stands and grabbed me from behind while jumping on my back. Security had to pull her off of me. My brother Kevin who had an Ease-Town Posse jacket on went to the rest room by himself and got mobbed. Big Rob had to go get Kevin and escort him back to where

We were. When he came back, he looked like he had been in a fight because his clothes were hanging off of him where the mob had grabbed his jacket, his pants were falling off and he had a few scratches where girls were trying to touch him. Now I see why stars need bodyguards. It's because some fans can be dangerous. After all the acts went on, it was time for the headliner, MC Hammer. Hammer's dancers were called 3-5-7. Me and Trouble (T- Roy, one of Heavy-D's dancers), were on the side of the stage looking at how 3-5-7 looked in those biker shorts. We laughed and joked about what we would do if we ever had a chance to get one of them in the bed. We kicked it backstage and said we would see each other around. Sadly, that day would never come.

Trouble (T-Roy) fell to his death in Indianapolis after

playing in an 11 story parking garage. That happened one week after we were just laughing and joking with one another. T-Roy, Rest in Peace! After the show, the promoter asked us if we would still perform on another show he was giving in month's time in Dallas. He asked if we would still charge him $4,000 like this time. And we said "like this time!" And he said "yeah, ya'll got paid right? I paid you all $4,000 for this show." You see, Ron, the guy in Atlanta was booking shows for $4,000 and told us the promoter gave us $1,800 plus hotel.

That meant that after getting on stage and performing our butts off, we were getting screwed out of about $2,200. Multiply that by about 6 concerts Ron hooked up for us…or should I say for himself and that would have been $13,200. Not bad for making a few phone calls and hooking up 6 shows.

Needless to say, we tried to find another booking agency to book our shows. One thing about Ron…he knew a little bit of everyone and could help you but screw you all in the same breath. And, if you ask me, Herk and Ron split that $2,200 every show. One thing I could not understand, I heard Herk say that he counted $800,000 one time. How can you screw someone who does not even have $100, and you just counted over half a million dollars of your money? After leaving Ron and his booking agency, the shows slowed down and the album sales were dropping.

Hammer & Louis asked us to meet them in Flint, Michigan to open the show for them. Now a lot of people felt that

MC Hammer was soft because he danced. I remember at the show in Flint, the promoter only had half of Hammers money and I guess he was depending on a large crowd to show but for some reasons, the crowd was not as large as other shows so the promoter didn't have his money. So he promised Hammer that by the time he got off stage he would have the other half of his money. Well, Hammer finished the show and the promoter did not have the rest of the money. So Louis and Lloyd, one of Hammers guards had the promoter hemmed up right in front of me. Louis asked the guy how much his Rolex was worth and the guy told him $15,000 and Lloyd took it right off the guy's wrist and also took the car keys to his brand new Jaguar. Before we all left the next day, the promoter came up with the rest of his money. Louis told Lloyd to give him back his keys and the Rolex.

Louis told Herk that when they came to Dayton in two weeks time, he wanted to sit down and talk business with him. When that show came around, Louis asked Herk how our record sales were and Herk told him that the momentum was slowing down. Louis said that since he looked out for him when they first started that he would help by signing us to a contract to Hammer's Record Label, (Bust It Records), and give him a percentage. Instead of letting Louis sign us, Herk tried to sell us to him. Louis said, "come on Herk, I can help them blow-up." Louis went on to say that we haven't sold a lot of records to the point where he should pay for us. He just wanted to help us become major players in the industry because he saw something big in us. After the word got back to me from Hammer's bodyguard Lloyd, that Louis made Herk an offer and Herk turned it down, it pissed me off.

Herk was not in a position to help us become gold or platinum artists. All he cared about was a front for his street game. When it was time to get royalties from the album, none came. 2-Pot would call Herk and ask when the money was coming from Jon Abbey, the head of Itchiban, our distribution company and he would say that Jon hadn't sent the check yet. So since 2-Pot was 50/50 partners with Herk, he would call Itchiban and Jon would say, "talk to Herk."

Now, my man 2-Pot and I had a special friendship. When I first signed to Bullseye, I told them that if I had to quit my job to go on promotional tours, all I needed was enough money for milk and diapers for my newborn son, Andrew, and money to make my car payment on my new Berlinetta Camaro. They both agreed and I signed the contract. When it was time for diapers, I would tell Herk and nothing happened. When it was time for my car payment, nothing would happen. Now after I told 2-Pot, he immediately took care of everything out of his own pocket. When Christmas came around, he gave me money to assist me in buying gifts for my kids and family. 2-Pot really kept his part of the deal and Herk did not. The sad thing was that they were 50/50 partners and Herk never gave2-Pot a dime back for his half. 2-Pot had a good heart and he helped many others besides me.

Things started falling apart after that last show when

ALMOST THERE

Hammer and Louis made Herk an offer for my group. One day, Bert, myself, and a guy named Big Red were coming from the YMCA after playing basketball and as soon as we arrived at Herks spot on Third Street and I got out of my car, I saw Herk at a car talking to one of his women. He gave her a brown paper bag and I said look at all of these cop cars coming down the alley.

When Herk saw them, he told his woman to pull off. As soon as he said that, a cop jumped in front of the car and told her to stop, then decided to let her drive away.

The next time I turned around, a police 9 Milli was in my face, he told us to get down on the ground. It was about 20 Drug Enforcement Agents everywhere. They searched the inside of Herk's spot. While we were lying face down, I asked him if anything illegal was in there and he said no, but he just gave his girl a paper bag with $50,000 in it. See, Herk had money, but a family member of his had a *whole lot of money*. I'm talking Big Boy money, millions.

After that incident, we went to Atlantic City for a Hip-Hop conference. When we arrived, we found out that the next morning, Hurricane Andrew was coming. They were boarding up the glass buildings. We stayed at the Trump Tower. Here, I met two legends of Hip-Hop...DJ Red Alert and DJ Chuck Chill-out. We performed that night and met a white rap group called 3rd base. They had just signed with Def Jam.

This is where all hell breaks loose. Later that night, Herk got a phone call that a lot of major players and dealers in the city got busted and a few of his spots were hit.

So he woke everyone that night and we piled into the van and went back to Dayton that night. A couple of days went by before I received a phone call from a Federal Agent; he asked me how much money I received off of the record sales from my album. I told him that I didn't receive one penny. And he said I don't know why not, when Bullseye Records account had over $183,000 in it. I almost dropped the telephone, but I stayed calm. So he said, "You mean to tell me that none of that money is yours?" And I said, "I'm sure a portion of that is mine."

Then he said that he could make sure I receive a nice little share of that if I told them what they wanted to know about Herk and 2-Pot. I told them that whatever they did outside of Bullseye Records, I knew nothing about, nor is it any of my business. He went on to ask me about my single album cover and who's Corvette I was sitting on. He went on to say that they have been watching Bullseye for about 6 months and if I didn't cooperate that I would also be facing charges. I told the agent that if they have been watching Bullseye for 6months,

then they already know that when we are in the office, it's all about the music business. And when we leave, I go one way and Herk and 2-Pot goes the other way. I guess he got pissed off because I wouldn't cooperate to bring down Herk and 2-Pot, and he told me to watch my back and that they're going to watch me. You see, I had nothing to fear because I didn't sell drugs or commit any crimes. So they would get sleepy watching me do nothing. After our little conversation, I paged 2-Pot 911 and told him what the agent told me. He came by to pick me up because he said that the phone could be tapped. As we rode around the city, I told him everything that the agent told me. He said things were looking bad and that he would talk to Herk about him letting Louis sign us so we can go on with our career. He said maybe we could look out for them when we make it big.

I have much love and respect for 2-Pot because once I got tired of being broke, I asked him to get me started in the street game so I can *come up*. He told me to stick to my music because the streets ain't for me. He said "God gave you a special talent, use it and in time you will get what's truly yours." I said, "that's easy for you to say, you just counted out $1.5 million." But one thing I realized was that 2-Pot respected me and my talent. Now Herk once tried to give me some dope to go sell instead of monies that he owed to me for record sales. We had a big falling out that day at the offices of Bullseye. I told him that I wanted what was coming to me and he said that John at Itchiban hadn't sent him anything. It has been 6 months and I'm sure he received some kind of money by now. Once Herk was out of the office, I started rambling through his desk and lucked up and found a statement from the distribution company. The statement showed that we sold 38,000 copies in one month. Now I know that they were getting at least $7 per album. So if you multiply 38,000 by $7, you get $266,000. So I see how they could have $180,000 in an account like the Feds told me.

2-Pot tried to talk Herk into letting Louis and Hammer sign the Ease-Town-Posse but deep down, Herk knew I was his meal ticket, especially when the Feds came knock'in. So he was basically saying fuck me and my career. About one week after that, all hell opened up on Bullseye Records. The Feds raided Herk's houses, his big money relative, some associates and many others. From Herk alone they confiscated 2 houses, $250,000 worth of jewelry, cash, a Corvette, a 750 BMW and a black drop top Cadillac amongst other valuable assets. Everyone in Herk's inner circle got hit all on the same day. 2- Pot was one of the only people not to get hit. See if 2-Pot did sell drugs, he did not do business with Herk because he knew Herk was greedy and disloyal. About one week after Herk was hit, other known traffickers were hit. A lot of people were taken in for questioning.

There became speculation as to why 2-Pot was not hit like the others. As for me, personally, I was waiting for an agent to come and knock on my door and take me down since the agent I talked to told me to watch my back. But, nothing ever happened. A week later, Herk's big money relative came into Herk's spot and I overheard them talking about 2-Pot. They wondered if he would talk to the FBI and basically rat on them. Herk shrugged his shoulders like he really didn't know and Big Money Man shook his head and walked out with a real concerned look on his face. I knew what that look meant.

ALMOST THERE

See, Big Money Man was an old school player who didn't take any mess and would do whatever he had to, to ensure the safety of his empire. Now after hearing this, I called 2-Pot and told him what I heard and he went ahead to talk to Big Money Man and got everything cleared up. Now, some people may feel that I snitched on Herk, but 2-Pot had looked out for me and I was looking out for him. That's how I get down. I'm loyal to those that are loyal to me. One day, I was at home watching T.V. and they had a news flash about a suspected drug dealer who had supposedly brought in around 100 Kilos of cocaine into the city. As I looked on...I saw the front of 2-Pot's house and then I saw several agents going in and out of his house with boxes, and one agent even dropped the top on his Corvette and rode out as if it was his own. They confiscated guns, jewelry, cars, houses, everything but drugs. They told him that they had an informant that was working for them and that he was going to jail for a very long time. I remember after I saw what happened on the news, I paged 2-Pot 911 and the Feds called me back and told me to stop calling this number because after today, he would be using a jail phone for the next 15-20 years. Now, after they hit 'Pot, they hit the Big Money Man. They told him that they had an informant who wore wire taps and that he would not escape prison this time around.

Now basically, the CEO & President were in jail for drugs. The doors folded on Bullseye Records and left me *FUCKED*. Now, after 2-Pot bailed out of jail, he tried calling Louis to see if we could get signed to Hammers Label, but they were on a world tour. He could have been in any country. When the Feds finally brought up charges against 2-Pot and Big Money Man on the signed statement of Money Laundering, Drug Dealing and a host of other charges, the name of the informant was none other than Herk himself. He ratted out everyone including his uncle, (Big Money Man), who was said to have gotten Herk started in the game years ago, he was the reason Herk was a millionaire and was able to buy $250,000 in jewelry, Benz's, 'Vettes and BMW's.

But all that didn't matter when it was time to go lay it down. He sold everyone out for his own freedom. Now, one thing led to another and everyone who was associated with his empire was locked up. 2-Pot was facing 19 years in prison if he lost his case. 2-Pot asked a lot of people to go to court on his behalf. No one wanted to get involved with a drug case. He told me everyone he asked to go on his behalf declined.

I told him that I would go speak on his behalf in a heartbeat. He called his lawyer; his lawyer called me and read what 2-Pot was facing and what charges they were trying to get him on. And one was Money Laundering, because Herk told the Feds that Bullseye was a front for his drug game and that Bullseye wasn't profitable. I knew I could be of some help because I still had that statement from earlier with 38,000 records sold equaling about $266,000. Now if that's not profitable…then what is?

My reason for going to court on 2-Pot's behalf was for

several reasons. (1) The company (Bullseye) was profitable. (2) To show him support and to show him how much I appreciated what he had done for me. (3) He became a close friend and he tried to do everything within his power to get my career off the ground. He was 50/50 with Herk but when monies came in, he also got zero. When it was time for court, we all stood outside the courtroom and said a prayer and then went inside. Once inside, they put Herk on the stand first and asked him if he sold drugs and did he sell any with 2-Pot and if so, how much? Herk went on to admit that he was a drug dealer and he and 2-Pot brought in like 100 Kilos of cocaine from 1988-1990. Then they asked Herk about Bullseye Records and Herk told them it was just a cover up and that the company made no profit and the money in the account was drug money.

After Herks statements 2-Pot's lawyer caught him in a lie. He asked Herk if he worked for the police and Herk said no. Then he asked Herk what they confiscated in the drug bust at his home. Herk told them and they asked if he received anything back. Herk said no again. See one thing 2-Pot did was hire a private investigator. He found out that Herk had been working for the Feds for about 6 months prior to everything jumping-off. After Herk said what he had to say, 2-Pot's lawyer pulled a piece of paper out that he had received from the private investigator and handed it to Herk and told him to read it. When Herk started reading the paper out loud, I could not believe what I heard.

It said that he worked for the Feds and that everything that they took from him in the bust was given back; even the $250 grand worth of jewelry. And every time he told on someone, whatever they got caught with, whether it is money or assets, he got 10 percent. That's one of the reasons why he told on Big Money Man because he had so much money, and he would get 10 percent of the millions he had. When it was time for me to hit the stand, they showed me pictures where we were in Atlanta at Jack the Rapper. They had photos of all of us with MC Hammer, Russell Simmons, Bobby Brown and Will Smith. They had my album cover and they asked me if the company made money and how I knew. So, I pulled out the old statement from Itchiban Distribution Company that had it in writing that for that one month, Ease-Town-Posse sold 38,000 records and cassettes totaling approximately $260,000 in one month. That pretty much sealed the victory for 2- Pot and his team.

After he was found innocent of all charges, he told me to come by so he could take care of me for looking out for him. I was broke as hell, but I told him that I didn't do it for money. I wanted to show my appreciation for the things he had done for me in my time of need. I told him that I just wanted to "be there for him in his time of need. We hugged, shook hands, said friends for life and I left the court building feeling good and bad. Good because I was able to be there for someone that had been there for me…and sad because that was the end of Bullseye Records and my record deal.

THE RISE AND FALL OF BULLSEYE RECORDS

P.S. Herk reached out to me via Facebook and we discussed our feelings about the Bulleye Records situation. After a long conversation, we as men decided to move forward and forgiveness was granted.

Groupie Love

What would a book be on a Rap Artist without a story about Groupies? Groupies and drugs are all part of the industry. I've had a few run-ins with Groupies on several occasions so I'm going to let you guys in on just one.

Mobile, Alabama was one city that really promoted and pushed my album and it was a place that made my group and I feel good about being in the industry. After our show, we headed back to the hotel with at least, 4-car loads of females following our tour van.

I was kind of tired after our show so I signed a bunch of autographs and headed to my hotel suite.

Once I entered into my room, I tried turning on my light but it wouldn't come on. Out of the corner of my eye, I saw something on my bed move and to my surprise, I saw two glow necklaces, (the green florescent ones you buy at a concert), and from the glow, my eyes widened even more when I saw two sets of tits under that glow. Yes, two pretty thick, chocolate Alabama babes were in my bed waiting for *Dr.*

Ease to operate on them. Now me being who I am, I grabbed a chair and pulled it up to the side of the bed. They had a 5th of Hennessy, a joint rolled up and told me to enjoy the show. After pushing play on a cassette radio that was next to the bed, I watched them perform on each other for about 5 minutes, because that's all I could stand, I had to join in and get some of that southern hospitality groupie love. Yes, I strapped up and put in work Ohio Player style on both of them. I was pull'in hair and smack'in ass straight-up hood style baby for about 45 minutes. I could get into more detail but this isn't a Zane book. Much love to Zane on her style, but I know young Artists will read this so I'm gonna leave it at this...*Dr. Ease* had a night he will never forget.

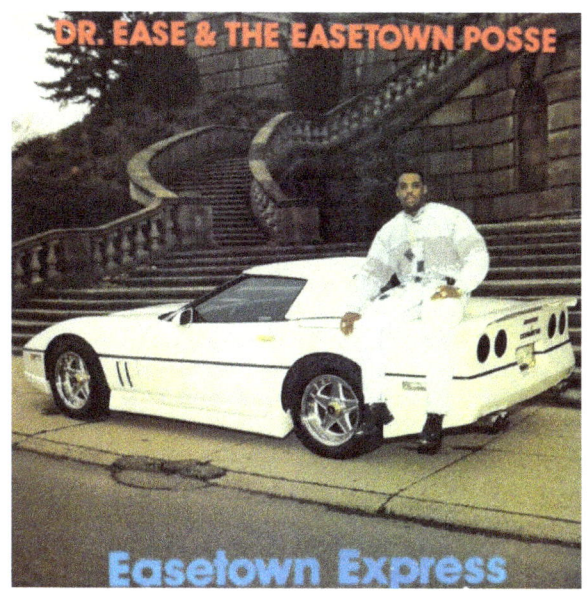

Dr. Ease Magnum 2-Pot

FIRST SONG ON THE RADIO

My first experience of actually hearing *my* song over the radio was unforgettable. It was a song called *Make It Last*. *Make It Last* was a slow rap song duet with a female named Madeline O'Neal. Her "Rap" name was Lady Lyricist. Lady L could hang with any female lyricist out there in the game. She wrote all her lyrics and they were hard. My man Darryl White, produced the music, we called Darryl "Old-E" because every time we saw him, he had a 40 ounce of Old English 800 beer. He originally made the music for his wedding. He gave it to me to write the words to his beat. At the time, Madeline and I were writing together. What we did was put a sample of Keith Sweat's (Make it Last Forever) over the music Olde-E wrote.

We wrote lyrics about making a relationship last forever. We took it to the studio and DJ Mix Sampled in Keith Sweat saying "Make it Last Forever" and that was how my first hit record came to be. After we recorded the song, we took it to WDAO Radio Station and a guy named Michael Ecton listened to it and then played it on air that night at 8:00 p.m. We told everyone we knew to listen to the radio at 8 o'clock because Michael was going to play my song. And sure enough, at 8 o'clock on the dot, he put our song on and I turned the radio up as loud as it could go and I couldn't stop smiling. I loved the feeling that I felt that very moment and I wanted to keep having that feeling. When the song was playing, my phone started ringing off the hook.

It was family and friends calling me to say that they heard my song on the radio. So many people called in to the radio station requesting *Make It Last* that Michael Ecton had to play it like 5 times on his shift alone. People kept on calling him to request that he play *my* song.

The song became a local hit. We even went and did a radio interview. My mother was a Social Worker at the time and I can remember her telling me that my song came on the radio while she was at work and her friend turned the radio up and said, "That's my favorite song". My mother told her that it was her son on that song, and her friend could not believe it. I knew that my mom was proud of me for making such a huge accomplishment. I felt like I was a major star because I had always dreamed of one of my songs being on the radio and at that moment, I had the feeling of one of my dreams coming true.

I felt like a college football player being drafted by a pro team. After that day, WDAO started promoting my song. It was being requested every day and *Make It Last* was in heavy rotation. I'd like to thank WDAO,

Michael Ecton, Jim Johnson and Marco Allen for pumping Make It last.

Fresh Festival

The Fresh Festivals were the most exciting concerts ever. I remember going to my first Fresh Festival sometime in the mid '80's and the lineup consisted of groups like, Whodini, Kurtis Blow, Run DMC, Beastie Boys, LL Cool J and some Break Dancers. I would go just to see how each performer would come out on stage. The one that blew me away was when LL came out of the sky in a huge 50 foot radio and when it landed on stage, E-Love, LL's right hand man pushed the eject button and LL was standing inside of the cassette deck. Then there was Dougie Fresh who came out of a giant globe, (he called himself the world's greatest entertainer).

And last but not least, there was Rakim and Eric B. They had a huge pyramid on stage and Eric B appeared at the point of the pyramid, opened the points and his turn tables were there. He started scratching, then the middle of the pyramid opened and a huge chair was in the middle turning in circles real slow. After about the 5th turn, when it came back around, Rakim was sitting in it. I remember when Kenny Wesley, James Scearce and I were on our way to Cincinnati to see a Fresh Fest and caught a flat tire on the way. By the time we fixed the flat and made it to the concert, LL Cool J had just left the stage. We had just walked in when a female in the crowd took one look at me and started to scream, "Oh my God, it's him" and she started to cry and her hands were shaking, and as I walked on to try and find my seat, other women came running at me crying and screaming. I didn't know what the hell was wrong with them until I saw another good friend of mine named Antonio Williams. He said man,

LL had on that same Nike sweat suit and Kangol. I said, "No wonder these females are trip'in." It was dark in the arena and they couldn't see my face, all they saw was the sweat suit. So my friends gathered around me and walked around the rest of the night perp'in like I was LL, just to see the reaction from the ladies.

That was my first taste of what it was like to be a Rap star. I always said that if I ever got to the point where I could tour with stage props, I would have a 50 foot hospital emergency entrance on stage. There would be sirens going off, fog all over the stage and a voice over the speaker saying, "Is there a doctor in the house"?

And then, I...Dr. Ease, would be lowered to the stage lying on an operating table. The doors to the emergency room entrance would open and I would rise from the table.........

Notorious B.I.G

I had the pleasure of opening a show for and meeting the great Notorious B.I.G at a concert we did together at the Memorial Hall. Other area acts like Jag and Toomb were also on the ticket. It was 1994 and Biggie's CD was blowing up fast. Once we arrived at the Memorial Hall, we were put in the dressing room right next to Biggie's. When I walked past his room, I looked inside and saw that he had food trays laid-out and a big bucket of Kentucky Fried Chicken.

ALMOST THERE

After we had gotten off stage, Biggie came over to my dressing room and asked us what clubs were poppin in the city. We talked and bullshitted for a moment. Now, I had about 7 other guys with me in my dressing room and every one of them stood over 6 feet tall except for my good friend, Jimmy Hat. Jimmy is a local comedian who looks a lot like Tommy Davidson. He stands 5'6" and weighs maybe, 120 pounds with Tims on. Now before Biggie went on stage, he asked Jimmy to watch his food while he was on stage. So while we all went to watch Big's performance, little Jimmy was standing guard at B.I.G's door watching the food. Big ripped through his CD with Little Cease and when he did the song *Warning*, the whole place went nuts. After B.I.G's performance, we all were kick'in it and I asked him why he chose little Jimmy, out of all the big dudes I had in my camp, to watch his food. And his reply was, "because I'm smart. I picked shorty because he don't look like he eats much. But you motha fuckas on the other hand…" He had a great sense of humor.

I'm glad I had the pleasure of hangin out with the great Notorious B.I.G before he was brutally murdered on March 9, 1997 (R.I.P). Now little Jimmy goes around telling people he was B.I.G's bodyguard and I say, "yeah CHICKEN-GUARD!!!!"

DARRYL T. EASLEY

Ease Droppin- Proper & Rugged "92"

STAR TRAK RECORDS

Star Trak Records was a small Black-owned independent label out of Baltimore, Maryland. It was run by a guy named Jim McNeal with help from two women, Ruth Jefferson and Glo Hunter. Ruth and Glo started D & l records under Star Trak Records. At the time, I was recording an album for Big Bang Studios for James Thomas and Keith Nash on Riverside Avenue. (They later moved to a house on Third Street). Big Bang signed a whole slew of local talent and everyone he signed had skills. Some of that talent included: The Dayton Cartell, Allen Fantroy (Capital P), and Mike Carter (The Coldest), Donovan Norvell (DJ Rip), RAA-K, JAG, Frank & Nicole (Lady Supreme). All of these Rappers were hot!

The one group that stood out was The Cartell. Capital-P had a style that I have yet to hear duplicated by anyone to this day. Half of his words did not go together or rhyme but it sounded good, like it all flowed together. The Coldest had a voice that was dead on Ice Cube. If you were to listen to his flow with your eyes closed, you would have sworn you were listening to Ice Cube himself. DJ Rip's production was Bananas. This was a group I would have definitely invested in. Sad to say, that Allen Fantroy (Capital P), was murdered by one of his friends. He was shot in the head with a Mac-11 machine gun. At his funeral, his father told me that I made his son's dream come true. He said that all he ever wanted was to be on a CD. I featured The Cartell on a song called Jack

Move on my CD Ease Droppin: Proper and Rugged. Now back to Star Trak Records. Glo Hunter worked for Itchiban Records when they were the distribution company for Bullseye Records, (the label I was on in 1989-91).

They were looking for a Rap group to kick-off D & L Records. Keith Nash sent everyone's product to the company and she remembered promoting my single, Make U Dance and decided that I would be the one to kick-off their label. Once again, I received a contract in the mail and took it to an Attorney, signed it and shipped it back to Baltimore. They paid for my production work and the album was complete. My plan was that if I "blew-up", I would help Big Bang recording artists to come-up behind me. While recording the album Ease Droppin,

I had a conversation with a guy named Craig Moon. Craig said to me, "Man…N.W.A talked about Compton, E-40 talked about Oakland…write a song about Dayton and Gettysburg Avenue". Gettysburg Avenue was our "strip". Just like Crenshaw in South Central, everyone would just hang out on "the Burg" and ride up and down the street just to have something to do. I wrote the song and sampled part of D.O.C's The Formula that Dr. Dre re-made from Marvin Gaye's song Inner City Blues. While we were recording the song, my Dancers, Bryant Bentley and Andre Lewis were hanging out in the studio. Andre started fooling around with the turn tables and a break beat accidentally came on and it was hot, so we put it in the song.

ALMOST THERE

Ease Droppin became my biggest selling album and the song, (same title), was a hit not only in my city, but in many cities across the country. I made #1 in Raleigh, North Carolina, Atlantic City, and Benton Harbor, Michigan. I was #2 in Philly and in the top 5 on a station in California. I received letters from all those radio stations asking me to come and perform and do radio spots for their station.

Ease Droppin was definitely a hit in my hometown. And at the end of the song, I added a lot of my close friend's names. They got a lot of phone calls from relatives from California or Philly saying that they had heard a song with their name in it. As letters from Radio Stations poured in, I felt that this was the album that was going to help me to take care of my mother and the rest of my family members. Star Trak started sending money so I could make a video and we could take it to the next level and do a remix for Ease Droppin. The first single was Ex-Chill Thing, a remake of the Dazz Band's hit Duzik, but whenever a program director listened to the album, they all started playing Ease Droppin. Then, the audience started requesting for it, so we had to give the people what they wanted and we rushed into the studio to remix the song so we could drop it as our next single.

While we were in the studio getting the single ready, Jim signed a group out of Boston called the Upbeat Boys. The group consisted of 5 white boys that could sing, rap and dance. Jim figured that he had a [New Kids on the Block]. So he stopped promoting everyone on his label, and started putting every dime into these guys. For example, my video cost $4,000 and theirs' cost $50,000. We had no promotional items, such as T-shirts, hats, posters or flyers. They had huge posters, hats, T-shirts, flyers, ink pens, pencils, book bags and they even had fucking umbrellas. I needed the umbrella because I was the one being shitted on.

I talked to a program director in Raleigh, North Carolina; because that was one of the cities that Ease Droppin was #1 in. The program director told me to rush him some promotional items so he could support us by using them as give-a-ways on the radio. He also said that we had one of the fastest growing singles ever, and that he averaged at least, 50 to 75 request calls a day to play the song. After hearing that, I rushed to call Jim and told him we needed promotional items for the station; he said that he was on another call and he would call back shortly. Two weeks had passed, and still no word from Jim. I called the company and finally reached someone. This someone gave me the full run down on why and what was going on with Startrak Records. This person said that Jim stopped promotion on my CD because he felt that he had everything he needed with this new group of his, and that by them being white, he would sell more records.

So the money he made off of the sale of my CD, he would put everything he had on the Upbeat Boys. The first thing that I could not understand was…how can you stop promoting a sure shot hit that the radio basically picked for you? The second thing was, how can you stop the momentum of a CD that was moving units and keeping the doors to your company open to take a chance on a group that has not sold one CD just because they are white kids? (Remember this is a black owned label). When I hung up the phone, I was basically hurt and upset.

After about a week of being pissed, I went to the book store and in every major publication such as Right On Magazine, Rap Masters, The Source and whole slew of others; there they were…the Upbeat Boys. After I made one more attempt to reach Jim, I once again talked to this anonymous person and he gave me more info on the label. He told me that Jim paid for a publicist to handle promotions on the group which cost a lot of money. Ain't that a bitch!

They get a publicist and here I couldn't even get a hat or a T-shirt. I can almost bet a million dollars that if Jim put one third of the money he put into the Upbeat Boys into my project, I would have at least, gone platinum and had a million records sold *fosho*.

After I didn't receive what was coming to me, I decided to pay Jim and Startrak Records a little visit (unannounced). I wanted to have a face-to-face with Jim and take a look at his books. My father talked to an attorney and he told us that we had a right to look at the bookkeeping of the label once a year. So I decided to pop in on him, (so that he would not have time to alter the records), and see how many CD's we sold. I wanted to know how much money I was owed. My father, Brian A.K.A *Bumble Bee* and I took an 8 hour ride to Baltimore, Maryland.

As we pulled up into the parking lot of Startrak Records, I saw a green Jaguar sitting pretty out front. I opened the door to the company and surprised Jim and his whole staff. Bee had a .38 caliber pistol that my father didn't know about tucked inside his waistband just in case someone got brave and wanted to act tough. After our surprise entrance, I confronted two individuals, Jim and Ruth because they were the two people that I dealt with. After I ordered Jim to sit the fuck down and start trying to figure out how to come up with my money, I ordered him to show me the books because I needed to know how much money I was owed. He went on to tell me that he made the biggest mistake of his life by putting every dime he had into the group, Upbeat Boys, and they had not even sold 500 records. He continued by saying that he had to file bankruptcy because he was being sued by the Upbeat Boys for breach of contract. I guess he thought I was going to feel sorry for his fat ass, but I wasn't.

So I grabbed an axe handle they had in the warehouse and put the handle on my shoulder like a baseball bat. Then, I asked him once again to show me the books. He said that lawyers had to be present in order for him to do so. If he would have stuck to his story, I would have felt a little better, but after a few more times of asking him, he changed his story to… "I would show you but my computer is down." [DING DING DING] Wrong Answer! I tightened my grip on the axe handle, and as I was about to commit Black on Black crime, I told him that I didn't come all the way from Dayton to Baltimore for nothing. And before I left, I was gonna have something to take with me. So I asked him for the keys to the Jag out front. Jim pleaded with me to understand his position that he had lost everything and had nothing to give me in return for my hard work, sweat and blood that I put into my project. Just when I was going to knock his head over the fence, my father stepped between us. I guess he saw the anger in my eyes because one second later and I would have done something I would have regretted.

It baffled me that a person could stop the press on a product that was rollin, and bringing in revenue to put everything into a product just because the group was white. I may be wrong, but it seems to me that if you have a product out in the stores that's selling, and radio is already all over it, then that's where you put the money. I asked to be released from the remaining years of my contract so that I could be free to work under my own label, and he agreed. Jim signed me off of his label and he then agreed that when I got my label up and running, he would distribute for me.

As we were leaving, we stopped in the warehouse and grabbed some boxes of CD's and cassettes and as I looked around, it seemed like all I saw was thousands of boxes of CD's, poster, T-shirts, umbrella's, book bags, pencils and lunch boxes with the Upbeat Boys logo all over them. I shook my head and figured that there was at least $200,000 worth of shit that was still sitting in the warehouse. I could only imagine how much stuff had already shipped out. Now that I look back on that whole situation, I can see how someone could lose their cool and kill someone for screwing them over. I guess it was not meant for me to go to jail for committing a double homicide in Baltimore over monies that a record company executive owed me.

My album Ease Droppin Proper & Rugged could have been a huge success and with the hot production, as well as hot lyrics and concepts could easily have gone platinum. We also had great reviews from major magazine publications for our production work on that album. If you would like to hear the album Ease Droppin you can go to DR. EASE MP3 Free downloads, and listen.

ALMOST THERE

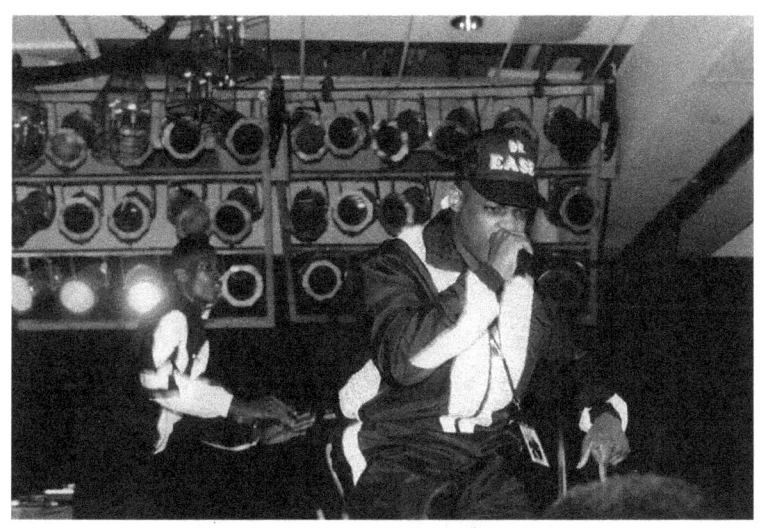

DARRYL T. EASLEY

ALMOST THERE

DARRYL T. EASLEY

ALMOST THERE

DARRYL T. EASLEY

ALMOST THERE

DARRYL T. EASLEY

ALMOST THERE

ROGER & LARRY TROUTMAN

Roger Troutman was one of the greatest musicians to ever originate from the Midwest. He wrote and produced great hit songs such as: *Heartbreaker, Computer Love, I Want Be Your Man* and the greatest funk song ever, *More Bounce to the Ounce*. I've had the pleasure of meeting and working with Roger and Larry on a few occasions. I can honestly say that on both occasions, Larry was an asshole with a capital A. I've always heard a lot of negative things about Larry, and the way he treated others but, I'm the kind of person that don't go by hearsay. And I am now here to say that I know on a personal level that he wasn't very kind to people.

On our first meeting in 1992 about a month before my second CD *(Ease Droppin: Propper&Rugged)* was to be released, I was on my way to Columbus, Ohio with my girlfriend at the time, Traci. We pulled into the gas station to get gas when I noticed a big light blue Lincoln Town Car that ran out of gas as soon as it turned into the lot. Being the kind of person I am, I approached the person and asked if I could be of some help, and to my surprise, the person was Larry Troutman. Larry said, "I would really appreciate it if you help me push my car to the pump." So while he pushed from the driver's side, I pushed from the back. After we got his car to the pump, I continued to pump gas into Traci's car. As I was pumping gas, I heard Larry cursing and looking into his wallet. He said he could not believe he left his money. So

I offered him gas money, and said, "Hey, you're human." I gave Larry a $10 dollar bill for gas and he said, "thank you, I really appreciate this and if you give me your address, I will send this money back to you because you saved my life."

I told Larry that I was a Rapper, and that I had a CD scheduled to be released in a few months, and if Roger ever needed a Rapper to [BAMM], Larry cut me off and said, "Man, I'm not trying to hear all of that shit, I just want to refund your 10 bucks." So I gave him my address and I wished that I could have siphoned the gas right back out of his fucking car because I did not have to give him a damn penny. And for him to be so rude to a person that he just claimed saved his life, tells you what kind of person he really was. I gave him my address so he could send my money back, and guess what?... IT NEVER CAME.

Every time I drove past Troutman Studios on Salem Ave, I wanted to go in there and ask Larry for my ten dollars. Don't get me wrong, it's not the amount of money but the principle of how he handled the whole situation, it's about the *principalities*. As if our first Meeting wasn't bad enough, our second meeting worsened the way I felt about Larry. Our second meeting occurred the following summer after my CD was released, (and was doing very well in at least ten different cities). The local radio station, U92 FM gave their very 1st annual concert called "The Fly City Music Festival." It was held at the Montgomery County Fair Grounds. My group was selected to perform at this huge event for the City of Dayton.

ALMOST THERE

The radio station also wanted to pay homage to the '70s funk bands that contributed to the funk scene in the music industry. The groups that were awarded were: *SLAVE, HEATWAVE, LAKESIDE, ZAPP featuring ROGER and the OHIO PLAYERS*. My group and I delivered a great performance, plus *Ease Droppin* was the most requested song in the city at the time. After our performance, Marco, the program director for the radio station, approached me and said that Roger Troutman wanted to meet me. I went over to Roger and he was standing by his tour bus. He asked me if I wanted to see the inside of his tour bus and I said only if I'm going on tour.

We both laughed and got on the bus. The bus was laid-out; it had a nice recording studio in it. We took a seat and he proceeded to tell me that he felt we gave one hell of a show, and how Dayton bred great performers. He asked me if I would consider opening a concert he was giving for Central State University's Homecoming. He told me that he was going to give it at U.D. Arena. He said the headliner would be *Queen Latifah* along with *Naughty by Nature*. I agreed... we shook hands and he told me to come by the studio the next Monday to pick-up the contract. *Zapp* came into the bus and introduced himself to me, got some information on me and I left. As I exited the bus, I said to myself that Roger wasn't as bad as I figured him to be. I thought he would be an asshole just like Larry, but he was a good natured spirit.

So in all actuality, face to face, person to person, Roger

Troutman was alright with me. The following Monday, my father and I went to Troutman Studios, rang the buzzer and was met at the door by *Zapp*. He gave us a tour of the studio, and as we went into the main studio, Roger was seated at the mixing board mixing a song that had all of his hits in one.

The song was called *Roger's Mega Medley*. He asked me what I thought about the song, and I told him it was great, advised him to add some hot hip-hop lyrics in it, so it could appeal to the younger generation, as well as the old school folk. Roger smiled and said, "I will remember that", and at that time, *Zapp* came and led my father and I to a small office. He wrote out an agreement, handed it to us and told us to look over it when we got home and then return it the next day. My father and I took it home, looked over it and agreed that it was fair. On Tuesday, we went back to Troutman Studios, chatted with Roger, and he took us to another office to sign the agreement. After the agreement was signed, Mr. Larry Troutman entered the office and asked Roger what was going on. Roger told him that we just signed on to open the concert for the C.S.U. Homecoming.

Larry said that the plans had changed, and that instead of *Latifah* and *Naughty By Nature*, they were going to bring *E.P.M.D.* and the *Hit Squad* that featured *RedMan*, *K-Solo* and *Das-Efx*. Larry asked me if I thought the show would turn out well, I said, "hell yeah, no doubt." Then he took the contract from Roger that we just signed, and tore it into pieces. He looked me right in the face and said, "we don't need an opening act for the show" and asked my father and I to leave. So I said, "Oh we can't open the show?" Larry said, "No, leave my office".

At this time, I felt it was time to refresh his memory on who I was, so I asked him if he remembered me from the gas station. His eyes widened and he asked me if I wanted my $10 dollars. I told him to go fuck himself as my father and I walked out the studio. On the way to the car, Zapp came out and apologized for Larry's actions and gave me 5 back stage passes for the show. I told Zapp that what had pissed me off, was that *they* approached *me* about the show. I did not come running to them. My CD was doing well without their help, and that Larry was a true asshole. The night of the concert was a disaster. Some C.S.U. students got real rowdy and started throwing chairs on stage. After E.P.M.D. tried to calm the crowd, it got even worse and the group had to run off stage and take cover. Fights broke out all over, and the arena had to call for police intervention. On my way out of the arena, I happened to see Larry trying to run for cover. As our eyes met, I just smiled at him and said "great show". That was my last face to face encounter with Larry. I saw Roger a few times since, and we talked a few times about music but nothing more. We had that industry respect for one another.

On April 25, 1999, I received a call from my brother around 10 AM asking me if I heard the bad news. I hadn't heard anything because I was at work that Sunday morning. He went on and told me that, the news said that Roger was shot in the back twice, and killed in the alley behind his studio. He then went on to say that they also found Larry in his car, a few blocks away with a bullet in his head. I was in disbelief that someone could do that to Roger. But Larry on the other hand.....I turned on the radio at work and heard the DJ say that it was ruled as a murder suicide. Larry shot his own brother Roger in the back twice after an apparent argument over finances and being fired as his manager. After he murdered his brother, he drove a few blocks away, realizing what he had just done, turned the gun on himself and blew his brains out. I'm going to let you all in on something… Roger was killed on April 25th, but on April 18th, he went to Solid Rock Church with Shirley Murdock and gave his life to the Lord. One week before his death. That's GREAT.

I even heard that he was about to record a gospel album with his nephew, Rufus. Throughout all the ups and downs, there's one thing you can't take away…And that is the fact that Roger and Larry Troutman meant a lot to the legacy of Ohio Funk and Funk Music in general. They accomplished a lot, and did a lot for the City of Dayton. My personal opinion about the Troutman's, and just my opinion; I feel that with the talent Roger had, and the firm business sense of Larry, they could have helped so many from the city of Dayton.

A singer…a rapper…hell even a country singer, just someone from Dayton. I'm sure whomever they reached out to help, would have reached back and helped someone else.

ALMOST THERE

The way I see it, is that they didn't have anything to loose and a whole hell of a lot to gain. [1] They had Troutman Sound Labs, a multi-million dollar recording studio. Therefore, it would not have been recording studio expenses. [2] Roger as a producer, was one of the most respected figures in R&B, and was seen as a god in the Hip-Hop community. *More Bounce to the ounce* was one of the most sampled songs in Hip-Hop history, and also kicked off plenty of careers such as E.P.M.D.

On the west coast, they called him "the godfather of funk." [3] They had all the connections to every major record label in the industry. So I personally felt that Roger and Larry could have profited millions of dollars more, by just reaching out to help someone from the city in which they called home…DAYTON.

P.S. I want to apologize to any of the family members who may feel that I portrayed Larry Troutman in a bad manner. But I spoke the truth based on my personal experience.

DARRYL T. EASLEY

Ohio Funk, 2002

ALMOST THERE

Ohio Funk Entertainment

After all the bullshit I've been through in the game, or as you would call it…"the industry", I decided to head up my own record company. They say the best way to learn is to go through it. Well I've been through it, around it, under it, and over it, so I figure that I have learned enough to at least give it a shot. Hell, I couldn't treat myself any worse than the labels I was under treated me.

Now I've always been a fan of old school funk music. I really had no choice growing up in Dayton, Ohio which was once known as the Funk Capitol of the world. In the '70's, Dayton alone was running the industry, flooding it with a new sound called Funk.

Funk exploded in the '70's just like Hip-Hop did in the '80's. The industry could not get enough of that sound from Dayton. We had groups like the Ohio Players, Slave, Sun, Heatwave, Phase-O, Dayton, Zapp and Lakeside. All these groups had hit after hit after hit. And all of them reached the charts.

As a kid, I looked up to all these groups at one time or another. After being fed up with the game after almost 20 years, I decided that it was time to do it my way. And if my way didn't work, then at least, I tried my best and would quit this game all together. I decided to call my label, OHIO FUNK for the love of my brothers from Ohio that laid the foundation for me. I put it down on paper from A-Z, and then I executed my plan to perfection.

The heart of my plan was to record songs with as many original Ohio Funk groups as possible. The way I saw it, if I achieved that, at least, all of the radio stations in Ohio would pump it. That way, I would at least, sale my goal of 50,000 CD's in Ohio alone. Then I would have had enough money to build a strong foundation. You see, if I could have sold 50,000 units, I would have made $10.00 a unit which adds up to $500.000…as in half a million dollars.

I also put together a staff to work with me at Ohio Funk. The personnel consisted of; my father, Ronald 'T-Bird' Easley as Manager, my sister Rhonda

Easley as Road Manager along with Mary Summers, Tiffani Richardson, Jaris Turner, Kevin Easley and Brian Ragsdale. Everyone had a part to play in making the company move.

I had set up a pay scale that was not an ordinary scale for staff. It would actually have paid my workers like artist. We were in this together and I wanted my staff to know that they were all integral players in the team.

I wrote out a pitch that we would say when we called Program Directors at radio stations. We printed up Ohio Funk t- shirts, and had plenty of CD's to give away. The first song I recorded was with the group *Slave*. I re-made their classic hit, Slide. Actually, I was asked to go on tour with the group back in 1994. It was an old school tour with groups like Lakeside, Confunkshun, Bar-Kays, DeBarge and Slave.

ALMOST THERE

The first city we hit was Minnesota, and then we went on to Kansas City. At these old school Funk Shows, you could tell that the crowd really loved the sound of *real* music, and they really got into the show. I would come out on stage at the beginning and hype the crowd, and then at the end of the show, I would close by putting a Rap to the song, Slide. The crowd loved the combination of old school & new school.

While on the road with Slave, I ran into Mark Woods from Lakeside. I told him about my idea of using one of their tunes. He gave me his cell number, and told me to keep in touch. Getting Slave in the studio would be no problem. We called Phil at Cyber Technique Studios, set the time, went over and did the recording. I had them play Slide's instrumental for about 20 minutes. After they left, I put the song on a CD, took it home and wrote a song called "Ohio Funk, 2000." After recording Ohio Funk, 2000, my mind was moving and trying to see how many more groups from Ohio I would be able to get together for this money-making project. The next group I wanted to get with would be the Ohio Players, mainly because they were the biggest group from Dayton. And I just knew that not one radio station from Ohio or any other city would turn down playing a song with the legendary 'Sugarfoot' on it.

As I was driving home from work one afternoon, I saw a man walking down Salem Avenue. The closer I got to him, the more I recognized him. I realized he was the one I was trying to find. That person was Sugarfoot from the Ohio

Players. I pulled over, introduced myself and asked him if he would consider doing the song 'Skintight' with me. He gave me his number and told me to call him the next day. I called the next day and asked him what it would take to record the song. He told me $5000.

I was heartbroken because I knew that I did not have $5000. But in all actuality, Sugarfoot is worth considerably more than that. And if I had it, I would have rushed it right over. I went on to explain to him that I did not have that kind of money, and if I did I would have gladly paid him triple that amount. I told him to let me at least, take him to dinner and try to come up with something. He agreed and on the following weekend, I took Sugarfoot to an upscale restaurant in Centerville, and we ate, talked, and just really got to know each other. When the dinner was over, *Sugarfoot* agreed to record the song with me. He told me that he liked my way of thinking, and that he once tried to get everyone from Dayton together but there were too many egos in the way.

As soon as *Sugarfoot* left my car, I turned on my cell phone and called Phil at the studio and set the time.

The funny thing about this whole experience happened when I went over to *Sugarfoot's* house to pick him up. He invited me in and as I sat on his couch waiting for him to get ready, I heard monkey and elephant sounds coming from somewhere in the house. As I looked around, I saw a bowl of spaghetti sitting on the table. He came back into the room where I was waiting and grabbed his spaghetti and we left. Now on the way to the studio, he fell asleep holding this bowl of spaghetti. When we arrived at the studio, he fell asleep as soon as we got into the lobby. Now I'm saying to myself, is he going to be ready to lay this track when the time comes? I went inside and got to work on the track.

Shortly after, my father entered the studio. After I finished the track, it was time to record Sugarfoot's part.

He jumped up as I called out his name and we all went inside the sound room, and he was like a whole new person. While at the studio, he taught me few things such as how to never be satisfied with what I had, and that it could always sound better. Even if I felt that what I had just done was perfect, he would say let's do it over. The song we recorded was 'Skintight'. Sugar, my father and I sang the hook on the song. After the song was done, we all felt satisfied with the finished product.

I would like to thank Sugarfoot and the Ohio Players for their support on the project. One thing I can say about this project was that I did something that has never, ever been done. I put the Ohio Players, Lakeside, Faze-O, Zapp and Slave all on the same project. That's history in itself.

My dream project took several years to complete. It wasn't easy because I didn't have the funds necessary to pay for the many hours of studio time I needed. I wrote, produced and arranged Ohio Funk, 2000. As a matter of fact, I wrote, produced and arranged every album I released.

I sat down and wrote out a game plan on how we would run the label and the people I enlisted to help were good friends and family members. The company structure was as follows:

- CEO-Dr. Ease
- President-Ron Easley
- A&R-Tiffani Richardson
- Marketing-Jarris Turner
- Manager-Rhonda Easley
- Road Manager-Mary Summers
- Secretary-Renita Lewis

I also gave a percentage of the company to Kevin Easley & Brian Ragsdale, (Kevo & Bumble Bee), for sticking with me through the years and going through the turmoil with me. I then created the logo with help from a singer named Sandra Curlette. She was the female vocalist for my label. I wrote out the shares and percentages for all employees and I incorporated my business.

Now the plan was to use singles with all Ohio Funk legends. The first single was called, Ohio Funk, featuring Slave, the second was Riding High featuring Phase-

O and the final single would have been Skintight featuring Sugarfoot from the Ohio Players.

As I stated earlier, I was sure that every radio station in Ohio would have supported my project by playing my singles. I mean, I had Ohio's greatest Funk Artists together on my CD…and with my flavor added to it, it was a win-win. I was wrong. What I didn't consider was that every radio station in Ohio was not owned and operated by someone in Ohio. I got more air play in other states than I did in my own backyard. I figured we could sell at least 50,000 units or more in Ohio with the right amount of air play. I was wholesaling to the stores for $10.00 per CD. They then sold them for $13.99 but I was guaranteed $10.00 per CD. If I had met my goal of 50,000 units sold, the company would have made $500,000. If I had been signed to a major label and sold 50,000 units, I would only have made around $350,000. And that's only if the album went Gold.

From that, they would have taken any money that I owed the company for advances, videos, promos, etc. I would have walked away with nothing. I thought that $500,000 would get my business off the ground but I didn't get the support from the radio stations that I needed; especially the one in my own city, (now off the air), and that frustrated me so much. After I got the structure of the company down and a plan in place, my crew and I took a flight to Atlanta to do some networking.

While we were there, we ran into Too Short, Jam Master Jay, (Rest in Peace), and a few other major players. To make a long story short, the vibe we left Atlanta with was that it didn't matter how good your music was…if you were not from the South, then they had no love for you. We met a lot of good people and coincidentally, met a lot of people from Ohio in Atlanta. This trip dropped my spirits even more and placed an even bigger wedge between me and the music industry.

The final straw came for me when I took a solo trip to Atlanta to attend a music seminar called Music 1.com in 2002. At this seminar, you had a chance to actually meet producers, lawyers and A&R's from major companies.

There were also a few artists there. They all sat on a panel and told us how they made it. They listened to our demos and gave us their phone numbers so that we could contact them after the seminar. It was kind of like a time to build a relationship with them. On the panel was: Johnta Austin, an Artist on MCA Records who got dropped from the label to make room for Tyreese. Johnta wrote the song, Sweet Lady that became Tyreese' hit song.

Johnta later wrote for Luther Vandross, Whitney Houston, Usher and a few other heavy weights. Jonathan Nyblack who worked for J-Records, Jon Christmas, a Black Entertainment Lawyer who also represented football and basketball players, a Black racecar driver, etc. And Stone Stafford, he was a major figure with Sony Music. He told us how he was the person that he used to look for when he had his singing group.

He explained that he knew how we felt. He knew what it was like to be struggling and trying to make it. He asked everyone to feel free to call him anytime. His seemingly sincere empathy made me believe him. That is until I tried to reach out to him and he wouldn't return any phone calls.

Another guy on the panel told us that if we wanted him to help us, it would cost $10,000 to shorten this up a little.

ALMOST THERE

The bottom line…no one on this panel gave a damn about anyone trying to make it. All they did was build us up and had us thinking that we could build a strong relationship with someone in high places when in all actuality, they did not give 2 damns about us and what we hoped to accomplish. They sat there and lied to our faces about what they would do for us. And as soon as the seminar was over…so was our relationship.

For some reason, that day was a turning point for me. That day, I decided to give up what I've been chasing for more than 20 of my 36 years on this earth. While I was on the flight back to Dayton from Atlanta, I called it quits. And I felt comfortable with my decision. In the past, when I wanted to stop, I would think about all of the people that told me not to ever give up. I thought of all the bullshit I had gone through and believed that I didn't go through all those circumstances for nothing. I thought about the promise I made to my mother of getting her a house and to my father of getting him an Excalibur.

To this day, people still approach me to ask if I'm going to release another CD and they express how much they loved the last one…Ohio Funk, 2000. With that CD, I accomplished something that had never been done and I feel that it won't really be a respected classic until I'm dead and gone.

Ohio Funk-n Out!

THOUGHTS ON THE INDUSTRY

It is my belief that the industry is designed to keep the Artist in debt. Here are a few examples of how the industry operates;

Let's say that you sign a major record deal and you get an advance of $250,000. Then you make a video that cost around $100,000. Next, add promotional items and other expenses for a total of $50,000. Now, we're going to stop right here, but there are many more money matters and costs involved that are geared to the Artist. But for the purposes of my example, we'll use the ones listed above.

That's $400,000 that you owe or are indebted to the company and your CD isn't even in stores yet.

Now, if your album is released and it bombs and you sell only enough CD's to reimburse the company $200,000 of the $400,000 you owe them and they don't drop you; you won't get an advance for your next CD. And because you already owe the company, you'll get $100,000 for a video and $50,000 for promotions

Money you owe company	$200.000
Video	$100.000
Promotions	$50.000
Total you are in debt	$350.000

This is what I call a financial crisis.

Now, let's talk about some of the Artists that fell prey to the industry. TLC sold over 10 million CD's with their CD entitled Crazy Sexy Cool, shortly after they filed bankruptcy. How can this happen you say? Let me explain how. TLC had a huge budget spending $1 million dollars on a video called Water Falls. They had clothes designers and professional hair dressers costing $1,200 per hair style. As a group, TLC made $.60 cents per CD sold. Having 3 members in the group, each person made $.20 cents each. In stores, their CD sold for $17.99 and as a group, they received $.60 cents out of the $17.99. Sad right? It is sad to say, but with the way the industry is designed, that is a standard deal. With the video alone, they were in the hole a million dollars.

Now in order for the Artist to receive any money, the record company had to recoup every dime before they start paying them their $.20 cents each. In other words, they had to sell $1 million dollars' worth of CD's to receive their $.20 cents.

Toni Braxton was also a huge star that sold millions of CD's. As a Solo Artist, she received $.35 cents for each CD sold and her CD sold in stores for $17.99. Toni's record company picked managers and attorneys for her that she did not even know. These attorneys and managers had the full authorization and access to her bank accounts. And apparently, they had full access to her money until she also had to file bankruptcy.

You can learn a lot from other people's mistakes, if you pay attention. In order to be in control of your career, you have to take control of your life. You have to know as much as possible about the business of getting paid in the game. You've got to know where the money comes from and how much of it you are owed. You can't be in the dark on financial matters. If you have a lawyer watching your back, get another one to watch his back.

Russell Simmons and Oprah Winfrey are two excellent examples to pattern yourself for success. Russell is involved in all aspects of his very successful business and I read somewhere that Oprah authorizes all checks at her billion-dollar organization.

The only way to really be in control in this industry is to start your record company and be your boss.

REFLECTIONS

When I tell someone that I am done with the music industry, they say, "How can you give up on your dream and let all that talent go to waste?" And I tell them that being a Rapper wasn't my talent. I could write a Rap for Oprah and if she rehearsed it and put it to music, then she would be a Rapper. My talent was writing the songs. Everyone can't write songs.

Presently, I am still utilizing my talent as a writer by writing this book. My life as a Rap Artist has come and gone and it simply was not my destiny to achieve fame and fortune as a big Rap star. However, it was my destiny to get into the music industry and have the experiences that I had. And as a part of my destiny, I have written a book about those experiences.

One thing that I would like my readers to know is that for each Nelly that makes it big, there are a million Nelly's that don't. There are many talented Artists out there that you will never know about. And that doesn't mean that they aren't just as talented as the ones that make it big; it just means that their destiny may have a greater calling for their talent. So now that you've read my book, all I can say is…take it for what it's worth. Be in charge of your path when given an opportunity. If you try something and it just doesn't work out for you, move forward on to something else and continue utilizing your talent. If things do work out for you, I'd love to hear you say that it happened because you took advantage of every opportunity that came your way. You knew what to and what not to accept. I'd like to know that you made it because you did your homework and studied the business… read up on the industry and took care of your business by not only understanding but also over standing the game. Then give all praise to God Almighty for writing your success into your life's destiny. And last but not least, you can say that you were *THERE* and not *ALMOST THERE*…..

Darryl T.Easley
EA$E

NEW BEGINNING

After completing this book, I developed a new form of music. It is a new form of expression that is just another way for me to display my creativity. I have never heard anything like this before and I call it Spoke-A-Nition. It's like spoken word but using definitions to describe the story. I perform this new genre of music under the name E-Specific because I am being very specific about what I am saying.

Introducing E-Specific

Coming 2016

Cover Designed By Elegant Stylz Portraits, Ms. Kym Russell

ALSO COMING SOON…My stage play;
"LORD, WHY DO MEN CHEAT?"
That I've Written, Produced & Directed
Throughout the play, I will explain why men cheat,
by using stories and scriptures from the bible.

Cover Designed By Elegant Stylz Portraits
Ms. Kym Russell

www.ingramcontent.com/pod-product-compliance
Lightning Source LLC
Chambersburg PA
CBHW050600300426
44112CB00013B/1998